The Sexual Spark

20 Essential Exercises to Reignite the Passion

By
Michael Krychman MD
&
Alyssa Dweck MD

Dedication

For John and Evan
...For the support, encouragement and putting up with our antics, endless texting and unique friendship

For "The Big Man"
...With love from a chip off the old block

Acknowledgments

Zane, Jace, Julianna and Russell may you all have excellent sex lives behind closed doors

But please TMI...Please do not share your details with US...we're still your parents! Thank your for retweeting without really reading!

ISBN 9781365053924

Table of Contents

Why Sexercise?

There is no time like the present to recognize and embrace the fact that that sex is not only for fun, or to express love and commitment or solely for procreation. While shocking to many, sex is actually a vital part of our general overall health and wellbeing. Yes! The emotional connectivity of a relationship is important; by the same token, the physical and medical benefits of sex are numerous and too often unrecognized and underappreciated. Some benefits are truly unexpected and others just plain awesome! Consider cancer prevention, benefits to heart health, enhanced immunity and improved mental health, to name a few. As gynecologists and experts in the field of female sexual health and counseling, we are consulted for advice day in and day out, from those facing physical and emotional challenges in the bedroom. "Boredom in the bedroom" is an all too common complaint. We need to reignite the sexual spark that has dwindled slowly over time. We are connected with our smart watches, iPhones, ipads, computers and other smart devices but somehow remain sexually dissatisfied and sexually unfulfilled.

With this in mind, we were encouraged to share our pearls with the masses. These "sexercises" are some the very tools we use in practice to help our patients find sexual self awareness and satisfaction, whether the journey is partnered or solo, gay or straight, monogamous or open.-We are all busy and have little time to devote to sexual enhancement- thus this book…to help restore vitality evolved. These exercises are easily downloaded into your relationship routine and are quick and easy to perform. They will revitalize your love life with sexual pizzazz!

We invite you to allow discovery of your sexual selves and enhance your sexual self-esteem. After all, sexual health is vital to general health!   READ ON, if you dare!

INTRODUCTION

The World Health Organization defines sexual health as a "state of physical, emotional, mental and social wellbeing in relation to sexuality; it is not merely the absence of disease, dysfunction or infirmity. Sexual health requires a positive and respectful approach to sexuality and sexual relationships, as well as the possibility of having pleasurable and safe sexual experiences, free of coercion, discrimination and violence.

The new concept surrounding sexual health is that positive sexuality is often attributed to overall general health. They are intricately intertwined. Sex has benefits that may have far reaching implications. Sex feels sexcellent and it will nurture your mind, body and spirit.

Sex Improves Your Heart Health

Sex can improve your heart, the ultimate love muscle. Your chances of heart problems may be decreased if you are having fun satisfying sex; in fact, the scientific literature supports that sex at least twice or more a week may reduce the risk of fatal heart attack by half for some men. The cardiovascular benefit of sex may be due to the orgasmic release of the hormone oxytocin that is produced during orgasm and sexual arousal.

The heart health benefits of sex don't end there! In one 2010 study, the American *Journal of Cardiology* reported that men who had sex at least twice a week were less likely to develop heart disease compared with those men who had sex only once a month.

Heart disease is the number one killer of women too! And her benefits may also be plentiful! Orgasm releases the same hormones!

Women who reduce the risk factors that contribute to heart disease such as stopping smoking and maintaining a normal weight and blood pressure, may also have improved sex and decreased heart conditions.

Don't get rid of your treadmill just yet but sexual activity is good exercise!

You certainly know that you sweat and may feel exhausted after sex! Yes! Sex is a good aerobic workout. You can burn extra calories with vigorous lovemaking. So perhaps you don't need to skip that cheesecake dessert after all when you are planning a hot love making session. It is estimated that the average person will burn approximately 4 or more calories per minute of sexual activity- that is 4 more calories than television watching.

BUT.... Don't cancel your gym membership or throw out those yoga pants just yet. According to a study conducted by the New England Journal of Medicine, for most people, sexual intercourse only lasts approximately six minutes and only burns about 20-30 calories.

Love your Big Macs at McDonalds?
Some British researchers have determined that the six Big Macs can be worked off by having good sex three times a week for a year. According to Women's Day magazine, add some caloric burn to your sexual adventure by   68 calories for an hour with kissing.   One Italian researcher discovered that that the mere act of taking one's clothes off burns about 8 to 10 calories.

A vigorous long lovemaking session can up to 200 calories per half hour.

Have an orgasm and maximize your caloric burn!

Bolster your Immune system with a romp in the sack!
Feeling sluggish or have the sniffles? The flu getting you down? Chronic infections or a lingering cough that you just cannot get

seem to get rid of?   Maybe sex is the answer!   Scientific research has proposed that human touch, getting a massage, hugging, holding hands, or even having sex -- all resulted in lower cortisol levels, which may be associated with lowered immunity.

Having sex, snuggling, hugging and intimate touch like caressing or holding hands causes release of oxytocin.

The Wilkes-Barre study from the University in Pennsylvania showed, that the close contact of lovemaking reduces the risk of colds. It showed that a significant cold-preventive effect for sex once or twice a week in a satisfying, long-term relationship.

Stressed? Sexercise to Stress Relief and an Elevated Mood.
Bad day at the office? Is your boss being annoying and demanding? The kids not listening and acting out?   Stress is surrounding us on a daily basis. Many people turn to exercise or yoga for relaxation while others turn to less favorable habits like smoking, drinking or getting lost in television or the Internet.

Sex can be a great stress reliever and it has the added benefit of maintaining intimacy with your partner. "Sexercise" releases feel good hormones like oxytocin and endorphins, which can help, soothe stress and decrease anxiety. Chronic stress can zap your sexual interest and libido. Testosterone levels, which have been linked to sexual desire in some women, can plummet during times of chronic anxiety and stress.

Sex benefits Gynecologic Health!
Women, who are sexually active and experience orgasms during their menstruation, may experience a potentially protective effect against endometriosis. Sex during menstruation also alleviates cramps and PMS symptoms.

It has long been recognized that as women age, their estrogen levels drop which makes their vaginal mucosa (lining) dry, pale, frail and inelastic. In addition, to using moisturizers and lubricants during sex, women who continue to be sexually active after they reach menopause, either with a partner or through solo self stimulation, may be less likely to have significant vaginal dryness pain and irritation. There is some truth to the concept of "use it or lose it".

An active sex life may help slow the aging process. Lowering cardiovascular risk, boosting immunity and decreasing stress are all vital components. According to an article in the British Journal, men who had sex less than one time per month were twice as likely to die within the next 10 years than those who had sex weekly. Duke University even confirmed similar findings for women! Women who reported enjoyable and satisfying sexual activity lived 7-8 years longer than those who were uninterested to sex.

To be fair we ponder the age-old question, of course, which comes first, the chicken or the egg? Perhaps those who have plenty of sex, lead a healthier more active lifestyle in general.

Either way, " having sex", it's a win win."

Cancer Fighting Properties of Great Sex
The Journal of the American Medical Association, reported that 21 or more ejaculations a month, were linked to lower prostate cancer risk in older men, when compared with less frequent ejaculations of four to seven times monthly.

Research has also found men who had five or more ejaculations weekly while in their 20s reduced their risk of getting prostate cancer later by a third. The impact on cancer need not be partnered sex only; intercourse, wet nighttime dreams, and masturbation, all count.

The cancer fighting properties of sexual intimacy do not apply to only men. In a 1989 French Study women who were infrequently or not sexually active, had a three times risk of developing breast cancer comparatively to those who were engaging in sex more frequently.   We think that both hormonal and brain chemicals (neurotransmitter) changes may play a significant role.

Sex is a Great Pain Pill

Can an orgasm replace the Tylenol or the aspirin in you medicine chest? Sexual stimulation can cause the release of natural painkillers, also known as endorphins. Researchers at Rutgers, the State University of New Jersey found that vaginal stimulation can help reduce minor chronic back and leg pain. In fact some women even report improvement in, headaches, or arthritis type pain with sexual stimulation.

Great Sex will enhance your Sexual Self-Esteem

Cindy Meston, from the University of Texas, "Why humans have sex," reported that enhancing self-esteem was one of the 237 reasons why people engage in sexual activity. Having sex may help you feel more attractive and desirable for your partner.

Sex can enrich your youthful appearance; boost your self-image and self-confidence.

Good Sex! Great Sleep!

Trouble falling asleep? Sleep problems? Sex maybe the answer to your sleep woes. The cuddle intimacy hormone called oxytocin is released during orgasm also promotes sleep. Oxytocin and sleep quality have been linked together in research studies as well.

Getting enough sleep has been linked with a host of other good features, such as maintaining a healthy weight and blood pressure.

Some other chemical reactions that occur after sex: Dopamine falls and prolactin can surge as well. These changes have been linked with feelings of relaxation, sleepiness as well as overall general satisfaction, contentment and happiness.

We are not surprised! In a 2006 Survey of 10,000 British men approximately half of them admit to having fallen asleep even during sex! So, before reaching for Tylenol pm, sleep enhancer or melatonin, why not give SEX a try!

Sex Enhances your Relationship and Closeness

If your relationship is down in the dumps it maybe because your sex life is lack luster. Sexual activity in a relationship can unify and act as glue to help preserve the intimacy or emotional commitment between partners.

Hugs, sex, orgasms all have been shown to increase the famous hormone of love, oxytocin! Also known as the cuddle and bonding hormone. Oxytocin allows us to bond, feel connected and also has the ability to help us build generosity and trusting relationships.

Sex Enhances Mental Health!

Researchers claim that satisfying sexual activity may be negatively correlated with the risk and incidence of psychiatric illness, depression, and even rates of suicide. Who knew?

Weak Muscles? Sex maybe the Strengthening Answer

Sex can stimulate, growth hormone to be released, and has been known to improve and strengthen and tone the pelvic floor muscles. When you orgasm, the muscles in the pelvis contract! Your stomach muscles, arms, thighs, buttocks also get a good work out.

Strong fit and in shape pelvic floor muscles improve your urine control and those strong muscles can help prevent incontinence (involuntary loss of urine). Some women will do kegel exercises when others prefer to engage in sexual activity. With an orgasm, your pelvic floor muscles contract!

Sex may make you smarter!

In a new recent study some scientists have suggested that sex can even make you smarter! Need a little help with a math problem? Do you have issues with work or feelings like you suffer from brain fog? Try a sexual interlude to help boost brainpower!

Great Sex! Huge Bank Account!

Who doesn't need an infusion of cash into their bank account? Sexual health maybe the answer. No, we are not speaking prostitution here. A 2013 Greek paper by Drydakis, examined whether sexual activity was associated with wages. They showed that increased sexual frequency was associated with wage return. Employees who were having sex more than four times a week received statistically highest wages. Some think that sex maybe a vehicle for love and connectedness and without it many people become depressed and isolated which will undoubtedly affect work opportunity and earning capacity!

Sex for Sex! Have it 2 times a week even if you don't want too.

Sex will boost Your Libido

Some women are reactive when it comes to their sexual desire. What this actually means is that desire may not be spontaneous but rather may be a result of being aroused and actually being in a state of sexual bliss.

Some women are sexually neutral- they can take sex or leave it. There is no internal off the cuff, burning desire for sexual arousal, pleasure or orgasm.

If you have reactive libido- arousal may be your starting point of sexual desire.

Yearning for a more sex? Sometimes it's best to just have sex even if you're not 1000% in the mood. Sexual pleasure and intimacy will be a great sensual motivator.

Sex for sex sake can improve your sexual desire and interest.

Having great sex may help you crave it more. It may boost your desire for the sexual reward of hormonal release and emotional intimacy with your partner.

How to Use this Book!
So now you are undoubtedly convinced... Sex is not only good, but it's good for you! It's not ONLY about quantity but let's concentrate on quality.

There is no right or wrong way to use this book. It can be used as a self-help manual or in conjunction with your sexual medicine specialist, counselor or therapist who may assign specific "homework" as part of your treatment paradigm towards sexual wellness. As you will see the chapters are outlined as He Said and She Said-! There are no rules. You can read the book from start to finish or random chapters in no specific order.

The book will evoke, promote and stimulate!

Thoughts will be easily translated into behavior!

We intend for these "sexercises" to breathe life back into a humdrum sex life.

Each partner should choose one exercise, and plan to execute the activity! Alternate! There is no set frequency. Some may find the time to do 1 or 2 exercises per month, others only 1 every once in a while.

Some Ground Rules
1) Don't stress

2) Enjoy the moment

3) Have fun

4) Make your love and sex life a top priority.

So.... Enjoy and Sexercise your way to sexual success!

Great sex is not really about luck but about attention to detail, making it a priority and committing to sexercise your love muscles!

Say good-bye to bedroom boredom and HELLO to bedroom bliss!

Take the Sexcellence Quiz.

Is your Sex life excellent?

Could it be more sexcellent?

Sexcellence Quiz

1. When you think of lubricants what comes to mind?
         a. Flavored coconut oil
         b. Scented massage oil
         c. KY jelly and astroglide
         d. WD 40

2. If you were told to read a sexy book you would choose:
         a. Fifty shades of gray
         b. The notebook
         c. The scarlet letter
         d. War and peace

3. What is your favorite position during sex?
         a. Missionary
         b. Doggy style
         c. Over the kitchen counter
         d. Asleep

4. Your bedroom is filled with
         a. A 4 post bed with handcuffs attached and a lock
         on the door
         b. Fluffy pillows, a comfy throw and a ceiling fan
         c. Pictures of your kids, grandkids and dog
         d. Your dog's bed, your baby's bassinette and a
         computer on the nightstand

5. Your ideal date night includes

    a. Sending the kids to a friends, mutual massages and romantic interlude

    b. Visit to the local dungeon dressed in leather and chains

    c. Early bird special dinner with the kids, nanny and in laws at Olive garden

    d. Working on your latest research paper

6. If you or your partner is dealing with pain during sex you should

    a. See your health care professional for an evaluation

    b. Load up on extra virgin olive oil because the economy size bottle is on sale at Costco

    c. Ignore it; it will go away with time and fingers crossed

    d. Consider oral sex- meaning, have a phone conversation with your partner

7. Sexting refers to

    a. Private sharing of erotic and proactive photos of yourself, and your genital by way on your smartphone

    b. Speaking sweet nothings to your partner on the phone

    c. The latest car rental company

    d. The latest fitness craze

8. Foods to get you in the mood include

    a. Whipped cream served up in the nude…. Use your imagination

    b. Chocolate covered strawberries and champagne

    c. Spicy Buffalo wings and beer….   Are you ready for some football?

    d. Chocolate covered crickets

9. Role playing refers to
    a. Dressing up as fantasy characters to spice things up in the bedroom
    b. Engaging in dominant/submissive bondage play
    c. Going to see the kids play at school
    d. Going to the bakery to pick up Kaiser rolls

10. A staycation is an amazing opportunity to
    a. Have a stress free, low cost vacation at home and reconnecting with your partner
    b. A great time to catch up on laundry and house cleaning
    c. Mowing the lawn naked
    d. Staying home alone and binge watching Netflix while eating a tub of rocky road ice cream

Scoring the Quiz

For each

A   4 points Great JOB!

B   2 points

C   1 point

D   0 point Really?

Points

Less than 10   Far from sexcellent
                  time to focus on your sexual side

11-25   hum rum/ho hum sex life
          there's more to sex than missionary

26-34   Satisfied but not quite sexcellent.... YET
          time to think outside the box.

Greater than 35
          Off the charts sexcellent!
          time to take a walk on the wilder side! You are
          adventurous and in tune with your own needs and
          those of your partner. You often implement
          techniques to combat boredom and are sexually
          open. Use this book to enhance and improve an
          already sexually satisfied sex life.

Chapter 1

She Said...

The importance of "Sexual" Medical Evaluation

WHAT is Sexual Medicine?

No, it's not all in your head! Sometimes, an underlying medical issue is to blame for the sexual complaints. While the obvious and most readily discussed and recognized is erectile dysfunction in men with diabetes or heart disease, for women, diminished libido, sexual pain and orgasm difficulties, to name a few, are intricately related to a laundry list of medical ailments, many of which are preventable and treatable.

WHY?

It should come as no surprise that sexual health and general health go hand in hand (if you skipped the introduction: that was the take home point!) and while the health benefits of sex extend well beyond the bedroom

> *Consider these fun facts: Regular sex:*
>
> *Relieves stress*
>
> *Boosts immunity*
>
> *Burns calories*
>
> *Improves heart health*
>
> *Revitalizes self-esteem*
>
> *Enhances intimacy,*

Reduces pain
Reduces prostate cancer risk
Strengthens pelvic floor
and….. helps you sleep better.
(Phew!)

So the reverse also holds true! Good sex Good health! Good Health, good Sex!

For example, identifying and treating low blood count (anemia), high blood pressure (hypertension), abnormal sugar control (diabetes), thyroid disease, menopausal symptoms, endometriosis, mood issues (depression and anxiety) to name a few, will greatly benefit one's sexual health. In other words, it's a two way street: better health = better sex and vice versa!

HOW?

Schedule a check-up with your healthcare professional. This might include an internist, gynecologist, urologist and/or a mental health provider or any combination of these specialists. A thorough history, physical exam and complete battery of blood work maybe in order and ignored by many due to fear, ignorance or laziness.

Newsflash: Prevention and Education might not only save your life, but may up your game in the bedroom!

WHEN?

Schedule a checkup. If your sex life has been zapped, ask for blood-work including a blood count (CBC), a chemistry panel (CMP), a thyroid panel (TFTs), a vitamin D level, hormones such as estrogen, testosterone, adrenal gland pro-hormones like DHEAS and prolactin, to name a few, and address any abnormalities. Don't be intimidated if your doctor is shy or appears embarrassed! Sex is important and seek out specialists who can address your needs. Make your appointments together and fine-tune the biological components to sexual health together!

Review your prescribed and over the counter medications that could impact sexual function and enjoyment. Antidepressants, anti-hypertensives, antihistamines and anti-anxiety medications are often ANTI-**sex**! You may discuss lowering dosages, stopping or alteration with the guidance of your health care professional.

The hormone havoc of menopause/ andropause, polycystic ovaries, diabetes, depression and certain cancers and their treatments can most certainly have negative effects on your sexual life and overall satisfaction. Deal with these issues! Do not deny! Ignoring chronic medical problems will not make them disappear and unattended to, they could worsen.

You are what you eat... as they say.

Nourish your body with a well-balanced diet full of fresh fruits, veggies, lean proteins and good fats, such as extra virgin olive oil. A Mediterranean diet is ideal. Portion control and smart choices are key.   Heavy rich meals are a sure buzz kill, especially on date night!

Drink! Drink! Drink? Water that is! Adequate hydration is key not only for excellent cell function and metabolism but also for prevention of those awfully painful calf and foot cramps during sex. Hydration enhances vaginal lubrication as well.

Limited to alcohol intake! Although it may give you the buzz, and it does lower inhibitions and possibly enhance desire or libido for some; it can dampen drive and increase risky behavior... not to mention pack on the pounds. Too much of a good thing is Definitely not a good thing.

Smoking.....   Just say no! Tobacco use is linked with poor health, diminished blood flow, yes even to the genitals, and thus less natural lubrication, not to mention, bad breath, ugly unattractive greenish teeth and earlier andropause or menopause. Need we say more? Who wants to kiss an ashtray?

Weight control and regular exercise to focus on a combination of cardio, weight and strength training all add to sexual self-esteem! They make us feel sexy, give us zip and pizzazz and brighten up our moods. The benefits of cardio far reach the gym: increased stamina in the gym can be translated into the bedroom.

Stress is a sexual deplete! Stress is a sexual drain! Meditation, yoga, paced breathing exercises and guided imagery are all highly effective stress reducers.

Chapter 2

He Said...

Let's look at Environmental Sexuality

WHAT is Environmental Sexuality?

Most of us have a sexual script; we have a preferred location where we have sex! Environmental sexuality not only takes the location where we have sex but also the sounds, smells and décor of our favorite sexual place. For most couples this is the master bedroom- it is estimated that most people have their predictable sexual interlude on Saturday night special after late night television is turned off.

WHY focus on Environmental Sexuality?

Sex needs a seduction. It craves a seductive sensual place to smolder.

We are all victims of our environment. When we fly on a crowded airplane with rude obnoxious people- we become anxious and angry. We are fighting for the armrest and our anxiety levels skyrocket! In a rush to work and end up behind the slow moving car- we start to feel our blood boiling. We are surrounded by stress! Let's not forget the smart watch, iPhone, bluetooth car phone, ipad and computers chiming endlessly demanding our immediate attention.

How about an escape into a luxurious spa retreat with soft music, warm glowing lights and sweet aromas? We can feel the stress also seep from our bodies.   Mind, body environment and sex are interconnected! Sex needs a calm warm and welcoming environment to smolder, then to catch on fire and burn!

HOW to address Environmental Sexuality?

Take a quick look around your bedroom. Is your room sexy? Sensual? Or is it a place of chaos and frustration. Now step back and take a closer look around the room.   Are there clothes piled up on the treadmill and chaos on your nightstand. Books piled up that are collecting dust? Are their pictures of your children or grandchildren on the nightstand?   Do you have loving pictures of your spouse?   What about the bed spread? Is it old and shabby, or crisp and sassy?

Colors? We can feel colors! Is the room dark, dingy or light bright and airy. Does your room smell like a dirty sweat sock or an inviting place for sexual intimacy?

WHEN?

This weekend plan a master bedroom make over! After you have done a survey, you and your partner should make a plan to transform your place of sleep into a den on sexual excitement.

Here are some practical suggestions

- Declutter- your bedroom should be restful and tranquil

- Put a ban on bedroom electronics. Smart phones, I-pads and computers must be banned! Cover that TV! Better yet remove it!

- Create a sex drawer (explore a sexual accessory shop and enhance your sexual pleasure with toys)

- Buy light dimmers at the local hardware store- soft mood lighting will set the sensual tone.

- Remove all pictures of children or grandchildren. We all love our family but these could be distractions in our sexual environment. Do you really want to look over in the moment of sexual passion and see your loving young child peering into your eyes! That may in fact dampen the mood!

- Are you bold enough- How about some erotic art?

- Select a scented aromatherapy candle together that is sensual and exciting for both of you.

- Consider redecorating- a new color of bedspread or some new pillows will recharge a humdrum bedroom.

- Stop by the music store or purchase a new music CD that will become your new sex tape! Something that is calming and excites the both of you. Better yet, allow Spotify or Pandora to assist with a sensual playlist.

Be creative and work together to transform the dull into exhilaration.

Chapter 3

He Said...

Write Yourself into Sexual Excellence with Expressive Writing Exercises

WHAT is Expressive Writing?

Expressive writing is a tool that is often used by health care professionals to help people come to terms with either positive or negative experiences they have had in the past. It is a way to conjure up sweet and loving memories of a time or occasion when you were sexually satisfied and filled with joy and love.

WHY?

Expressive writing is a technique that is used to help rekindle memories. By sitting quietly and focusing on past experiences one can vividly remember the pleasurable experience and while not trying to recreate that experience it may enhance emotions and feelings.

Expressive writing has been used in many facets of healthcare and has shown to address trauma and has demonstrated a reduction in stress-related visits to the doctor, improved immune function, enhanced mood and wellbeing.

HOW?

You will each need a pad and pen or pencil

Plan on 1-2 sessions over the next 2 weeks

Each session will last 10-15 minutes

Plan for some quiet time when you will not be interrupted or disturbed.

WHEN?

Over the course of the next 1-2 weeks take some quiet time, and plan for about 3-4   sessions of 10- 15 minutes each, to sit down and reflect

You and your partner will do this exercise separately then come together and share your thoughts.

Focus on your most satisfying sexual interlude with your partner. Take a pad and pen and think about a specific sexual encounter that was mind blowing, dynamic and swing from the chandeliers exciting! Was it your honeymoon? Sex in an elevator? Or that quickie last week? Sex in the kitchen?

Each of you will write down your very deepest thoughts and

feelings about the most sexually charged experience.

Focus on the What!
    What are details?
    What were we wearing?
    Doing? Saying?
    Hearing?
    Smelling?
    Feeling?

Focus on the Why?
    Why was it so special?
    Why am I remembering this experience?
    Why is it so important?

In your writing, there are no rules, no right or wrong. Do not worry about spelling or grammar. Sentences can be long or short. It may even be just phrases or words

You should plan to let go and explore your deepest emotions and thoughts.

After you are done with the 3-4 sessions, it is now time to share your thoughts with your lover. Sit down in a quiet space and share your erotic experiences remembered!

Remember the past, so we can shape our futures!

As you hear and experience each other's erotica remember,

Stop and think.... Yes it is me in that story! I am a sexual vixen!

Allow yourself to experience the sexual pleasure to rediscover your sexual self.

Chapter 4

He Said...
Body Map Yourself to a Sexual Dynamo!

WHAT is Body Mapping?
Great sex comes from discovery and self-awareness. Dr. Zoldbrod was instrumental with the discussion of body mapping and its use in sexual vitality. Very often we think we know what we like sexually and what rocks our sensual world. Most of us think we are in tune with our sexual pleasure zones and the way we can turn on our partners.

More often than not, we are wrong, incomplete, or our list of wants, needs and the details of our sexual repertoire, go unspoken and unacknowledged. We often do not want to be vulnerable and exposed by discussing our sexual secrets or hidden wants and needs.

Most people forget that the entire body can be erotic and sensual. Men are often the culprits too! The genitals are certainly dynamic and vital and shouldn't be ignored but most of us forget that there are many other areas of the human body that can be exceptionally erotic and sexually pleasing.

WHY create an erotic map yourself or your partner?

Creating an Erotic Body Map can unlock the mystery of sexual pleasure. It can help both you and your partner on the journey of sexual awareness and excitement. Discovery of new and vital body parts can give you great pleasure.

It is not uncommon for both men and women to find many parts of their body erotic. Discovery of a new erotic area can intensify arousal – rekindle lust and pleasure. It may even bring new untapped feelings of sensual excitement and titillation. Sparks may ignite! Touching and stimulating new areas can discover a hidden passion and create a longing. Novelty and discovery will fuel your desire.

Creating your personal map of desire and excitement can enhance and revitalize sexual communication between you and your partner. We often think they like what we are doing ... but do we really know? We may be embarrassed to verbalize our wants and needs and the Erotic Body Map is a good segue to this discussion.

HOW does one complete a body map?

Create

An outline of the front and back of human body on a piece of paper. It can be rough sketch and artistic skill is not important.

Color

Next take colored pencils and or crayons and fill in areas of the body drawings that you want touched, played with and enjoyed.

Let your inhibitions come down, explore and share with your partner through color and design.

A color scheme that some find helpful is

RED: IT'S HOT! I'm burning for this area to be touched and explore!

BLACK: IT'S NOT- please stay away from this area.

YELLOW: Proceed with caution but allowable and welcome.

Some other colors choices are similar to a traffic light:
Red- Stop
Green- GO!
And Yellow is yield or. ...proceed with caution.

Each of you should complete your own maps in private, alone. Sharing this exercise is the next step. When you have some time plan to share your colored map with your partner!

Maybe just put it in a decorated envelope and be sure to include your decoding color code.

Allow some time for each of you to absorb and review.

Try to give the map in the morning and plan to discuss it over dinner!

Then let the fun begin.

Communicate and Talk!

Be open and honest.

You will be amazed at what you discover! Let the sexual boundaries fade! It is ok to admit you love your toes caressed or even sucked! Or your nipples sucked and stimulated.

Focus on communicating your sexual wants and needs to each other.

When does Body Mapping Happen?

Over the next few weeks plan on putting your newly created body map into practice. Try some of these suggestions

Connect and Caress

Spend some time in sensual massage. Explore new areas of sensual erotica- you may re-ignite some electrifying feelings.

Set the stage by going to the store buy scented body lotion or love oil and plan an erotic sensual massage.

Start slowly with getting undressed and take a nice hot shower – either alone or together. Next, start with some sensual touch – and avoid the genitals, breast or penis- start with the arms, legs or chest and then get to the erogenous zones you have decided upon.

Take turns giving and receiving sensual pleasure. Enjoy the journey.

Kiss

Spend 5 minutes each day.... REALLY DEEP SENSUALLY KISSING, Not the standard peck on the check. Kiss each other with your eyes open. Rediscover the passion of kissing and sensuality. Not only kiss the mouth but also explore each other's touch and feel with your lips and mouth. Enjoy the sensual pleasure of tasting each other

Explore

Touch, nipple and stroke new body parts that you may have neglected. Break out of your comfort zone. Massage, lick, savor or delicately nibble! Tease every sensual area! Get your partner red hot and ready for new areas of pleasure. Nurture your hunger for sexual exploration and re discover your erotic sexual self.

Repeat:

You may want to consider redoing your body maps from time to time. Maybe it can be helpful to repeat it every few months. Some areas may turn colors! Enjoy the journey or the evolving aspects of sexual expression.

Chapter 5

She Said...
Practice Focused Sensual /Sensate Touching

WHAT?

The sensual date has its origins from the therapy couch. The sensual date focuses on specific touching exercises. The sheer experience of extreme pleasure and sensual awareness is the ultimate goal; focus on the journal of sexual pleasure rather than on orgasmic relief. Partners take turns touching the other and providing positive and negative feedback to each other. Building trust and intimacy are inherent. This technique is designed to reduce anxieties about reaching orgasm by focusing purely on what feels good rather than orgasm as an end result. Sensate focus exercises are ideal to treat male erectile issues or erectile dysfunction (ED), low desire and orgasm difficulties with the eventual hope that a couple may ultimately resume pleasurable and successful intercourse again. In addition, we often recommend sensate focus exercises for couples to reengage reignite and reinstitute mutual trust. It is a good prelude to rekindle the passionate flame.

WHY?

Sensate focus is a therapy technique used to explore intimacy and to increase awareness of one's own and one's partner's sexual needs.   Since orgasm is not the primary goal, these exercises help to overcome the fear of failure, disappointment or even disapproval that may have occurred in the past.

HOW?
Exercises are typically done in 4 stages over a period of several weeks.   See what your schedule can handle.   Sometimes meeting for 2-3 times/week may be helpful to actually see some progress.

Roles:
Toucher: One person starts as the touch master- they are in charge of giving pleasure by touch

Receiver: One person will be the receiver of sensual touch and be the one enjoying.

Partners can stay at one role for a session or may even switch roles after 20 minutes.

Don't forget to set the stage before starting.   Consider a light meal, a warm shower and an inviting sensual environment.

Once the stage is set, you're ready to begin...

During stage 1, touch can occur anywhere except the vagina, breasts, penis and scrotum area. Stay away from the erotic genitals! The toucher may want to uses his/her non-dominant hand or a softer touch with the dominant hand. The goal is to experience intense pleasure, but not to intentionally sexually arouse your partner or have an orgasm.

In stage 2, repeat stage 1 and then then begin exploring the breasts and genitals, but intercourse is off the table... You should enjoy the pleasure or erotic arousal and should not attempt intercourse, or excessive excitement that may lead to orgasm. Tease and enjoy! Use your hands, feet and even your mouth to entice and please.

In stage 3, engage in mutual touching, beginning with stages 1 and 2, and then move onto heavy petting or genital touching. Even if you both become sexually aroused, you should try not to engage in touching that might lead to orgasmic release.

In stage 4, repeat 1, 2, and 3 and let your excitement culminate and then you can then progress to partial or full intercourse or touching or even mutual oral sex that may lead to orgasm.

WHEN?

Try for several times a week to accomplish this exercise.
Set the stage.

Consider dim lights, subtly scented candles and soft music and a light meal beforehand.

Some enjoy the new candle/ lotion combo. You light the candle and then can drip the hot wax, which has liquefied onto your lover and use as soothing erotic oil.

Mood music?

Lock the master bedroom door! Insure privacy.

Take a bath or shower beforehand alone or together to ease tension and provide relaxation.

Establish whether you and your partner will remain clothed or undressed; whatever is more comfortable.

Massage oils are warmed, edible are always FUN!

Limit conversation until the exercise is completed. Try to communicate with soft moans and groans or other nonverbal communication. Remember to explore all your erotic areas! After the session you may discuss what was accomplished, positive and negative feelings.

Chapter 6

He Said...

Focus on Effective Sexual Communication

Are you speaking the same language of love, sex and appreciation?

WHAT are communication exercises?

Communication exercises help enhance the emotional bond between you and your partner. You share, breakdown barriers and begin to learn how to connect on a higher and deeper plane. Communication and trust often go hand in hand and will elevate your relationship to a feeling of honesty and connectedness.

You are no longer just two ships passing in the night but have merged into one cruiser on a mutual sensual journey.

WHY?

One of the most troublesome issues that modern couples face is communication breakdown. We have forgotten how to interact on a personal and intimate level. We often communicate while distracted, or focus on primarily on operational issues like the mortgage, finances or the children. We have become the texting, sticky note, emailing communication generation.

We neglect to remain in sync with our partners and this may create emotional distance between lovers. Somewhere along the timeline, we stop sharing and then worst of all we stop listening!

This emptiness of poor communication can lead to sexual disconnect and avoidance. Men and women want an emotional and physical sexual bond.

Communicate to connect.

Connect to enhance sexual dynamism!

HOW?

Communicate with Attention:

Communication requires attention to your partner. Turn off all potential distractions (that means anything with an i. iPhone, itouch, ipad, iwatch etc.) that may be limiting your ability to focus on the conversation that is happening. Chirping electronics like televisions, blackberries, IPADs and smart phones, chime or vibrate in the background, and create distraction and interrupt connectedness.

Communicate with Focus:

Stay focused on your partner when discussing important issues. Yelling from room to room without direct eye-to-eye contact undermines and destroys communication. Body language can also help tell your story!

Communicate with Fairness:

We speak with strangers in a nicer tone than we often do with our loved ones.

> Practice humility and respect.
> Speak in a low loving soft tone.
> Never raise your voice.
> Practice acceptance

Communicate with Equality:

People have different opinions and styles when it comes to communicating. Everyone should have an opportunity to speak uninterrupted and be heard. Active participation is encouraged. Try to accept and not argue! Use key phrases like " This issue is important to me" to draw your partner in.

Communication from a Place Of I:

When you are communicating speak from a place from "I". When you speak and focus on discussing how your partner or spouse makes you feel, it may come across as critical and aggressive. Try saying... I feel that I am not getting enough attention rather than say... You are always busy and not giving me what I need.

WHEN?

Three times over the next 2 weeks plan to perform the same if not all of the suggested exercises. Each communication exercise should take no more than 10-15 minutes.

Suggested Verbal Communication Exercises:

Sit face to face uninterrupted and take turns defining the following terms
   a. What does Love mean to me?
   b. What is Marriage?
   c. What is intimacy?
   d. What is Sex?

Defining these terms to each other will build bonds of love and togetherness.

Share and Connect!
   Intimate Sharing of Sexual Yearnings!

Each of you takes a piece of paper and separately writes down

Your personal sexual turn on's.

Your personal turn offs.

What you perceive the turns on are for your partners

What you perceive the turns off are for your partner.

After completing this solo exercise, come together and review your answers.

Together.   Share and Listen!

Discuss the similarities and differences. You may be surprised or have an eye opening revelation!   You will discover some unexplored sexual adventures, and demolish some sexual myths!

Physical Communication Exercises
You cannot always talk your way out of a sexual rut. Sexual RUTS are when your are when sex has become (Routine... Unimaginative and Tiresome!)

Non-verbal communication can teach us of an alternative ways to express love.

Try these physical interaction exercises, which can enhance your understanding of cooperation. It can also explore feelings of power and control. You will explore your dominant side and what it is like to be or submissive. Connect and communicate with touch and trust!

Both you and your partner should be ABSOLUTELY silent during the physical exercises. Make time afterwards to discuss the experience and your feelings

1- One partner should lead the other (who is blindfolded) around the room.

    a. Take turns at being the leader and follower.

2- Fall backwards into awaiting arms

3- Stand face-to-face, eyes closed, and push each other with open hands.

4- Sit across from each other, hands touching, and try to mirror each other's movements

5- Consider a 3-legged walk on the beach or in the park

Chapter 7

He Said...

Mindful or Mind Full- What kind of sex are you having?

WHAT is Mindfulness?

Mindfulness is the Buddhist tradition of deliberately paying close attention and focusing with undistracted quiet concentration. Mindfulness allows us to stay focused with a non-judgmental accepting attitude. You become consciously aware of your thoughts: the good pleasurable ones, as well those that maybe negative and self-defeating. Mindfulness allows you to remain in the present moment.

Mindfulness can help you feel, think and react in an accepting and relaxed fashion without negativity. Negative thoughts may float through your brain without cause or incidence. You choose to remain focused on the positivity. You are balanced, focusing your wisdom and moving towards an understanding of acceptance.

WHY?

Have you ever started driving to work and forget what stores you pass on your route? You have taken this road countless times. Has your mind tuned off? Turned out? Is it on autopilot? What about when you are eating your dinner …. before you know it, the plate is empty? Have you really tasted the food? We are HUMAN DOINGs, NOT HUMAN BEINGS! We are busy doing, not being! We have become mind full. Not mindful. We are the ultimate multitaskers.

We cook, clean, empty the dishwasher, raise children and work both in the home and out of the home with social responsibilities. We squeeze in the gym for fitness. We network with our peers, answer countless emails, and often forgo a few days of personal vacation. We are overworked and spend countless hours in rush hour to and from work in traffic! Our minds are always busy, calculating, planning and executing a series of activities to maintain the well-oiled machine on track. Preplanning almost every activity.

Our schedules are FULL.

Our minds are FULL.

HOW?

Try to practice little snippets (2 to 3 minutes) of mindfulness each and every day. It will take practice and perseverance. It may be difficult at first and you may find your mind wondering. It will wander to what you have been thinking about, worrying about or trying to figure out what you need to accomplish next. Remember that practice makes perfect! Mindfulness is often a progressive activity. Start off slow, with short periods of time and then progress to increase your time and activities.

Do not be discouraged as it may take some time to master the art of staying focused!

WHEN?

Everyday moments lend themselves to mindfulness. Try mindful driving- drive in quiet and focus on the road! Really focus. May be go on a mindful walk and really absorb the beauties of nature and the great outdoors.

Others may try mindful dishwashing… feel the texture of the soap, the bubbles, the warmth of the water and the squeakiness of the clean dishes as you rinse them

Start with just 2-5 minutes of quite time and focus on your breathing, the in and out of the breathe filling and leaving your lungs. Practice mindful breathing, paying attention to the thoughts that are passing through your mind!

Once you have mastered the beginning phases of mindfulness, it may be time to try a more advanced activity. You can choose any activity! Consider a detailed adult coloring book. A Mandala coloring book can be a soothing way to spend a mindful afternoon) as a mindful exercise.

Mindful Eating

In the middle of an eating a meal, start by paying attention to your breathing and chewing, focus on the sounds or the sensations, sights or thoughts while chewing your food. Savor each moment. Be aware of your breathing and allow yourself to full experience the food you are eating. Understand and appreciate the texture of the food, the smell and the taste as you chew and finally swallow! Appreciate the new sensations and flavors. Do not rush.

Mindful Sex

Mindfulness training when done during sexual activity can enhance our sexual pleasure and bring our sexual experience to a new level of euphoria and excitement. It may be challenging to stay focused during sex. We are constantly being bombarded by potential interruptions: Are the toddlers walking around? Is that the phone ringing or has the smart phone just signaled a new incoming email or text? Maybe it is important? Are the teens home.... Was that really the garage door opening?

Stack the deck in your favor. Plan your sexual interlude when interruptions will likely be at a minimum, remove technology from the bedroom and silence the electronics. Use the master bedroom lock to ensure uninterrupted privacy. During sexual activity pay attention to how your body is reacting, enjoy the sensations, and relax while consuming the feelings of arousal and pleasure. Notice both the positive and negative feelings you may be experiencing but let them just drift out of your mind as you regain focus on the pleasure reaction all over your body! Pay attention to the sexual feelings pulsating through your entire body.

Focus on your sexual energy and vitality.

Mindful sex will transform sex into a mutually satisfying and dynamic encounter filled with sensuality, indulgence and love.

Chapter 8
She Said...
Read Books and Watch Movies to Enhance Sexual Excitement
the Benefits of Bibliotherapy and Erotic Movies

What?

Sometimes we get so bogged down with the hum drum day to day responsibilities of work, kids, finances, and family issues, spontaneous thoughts about sex and fantasy can be fleeting and even nonexistent. Engaging in erotic reading or watching sexy movies is beneficial to your sexual life. Women who read erotica have more spontaneous sexual thoughts and more satisfying sexual behavior than women who don't! Do we even need to go on? Sexy books, sexy thoughts!

Of course, women who have regular sexual thoughts may be even more sexually engaged to read erótica.

Why?

Bibliotherapy, or the reading of books or articles with sexual content, are known to   promote sexy thoughts and invite fantasy and even the forbidden into your consciousness. Getting lost in a suggestive or erotic story is a temporary escape from the mundane and ordinary antics of the typical day to day.

Keep in mind, it is perfectly normal to get "turned on" by the erotic whether in print or on screen. Just because you enjoy reading about a particular sexual fantasy doesn't mean you are a strange wierdo or that you even want to experience these fantasies in reality!

How?

In practice, we often recommend structured homework for those having few to no spontaneous sexual thoughts and fantasies.

Suggestive reading or vídeo watching is advised three or four times per week for 10- 20 minutes per session. The purpose is to encourage and promote "sex on the brain"

When?

Here are some pearls for success:

During your reading, you should have uninterupted privacy and be free from of interruption by kids, phone or time constraints. Both you and your partner can take turns reading to reach other or read your own privately! Snuggle in bed while reading.. Watch a fun dirty movie; alone or together and watch the sparks fly!

Commit to at least 20 minutes 3-4 x weekly

Choose reading material that is in sync with your comfort level. This could include instructional, fantasy, romance or graphic pornographic material.

Once you find a topic, genre or author you are comfortable with, paruse amazon.com or Barnes and Noble for similar selections.

Literotica.com is another amazing online resource. The options are abundant and will fit any tastes or fancy.

Erotic, romantic, fantasy or pornographic movies can also be introduced into your relationship! . Consider choosing some movies with your partner!

Shopping for erótic books or movies together can open the door for communication and enhance discussion. This is ideal to consider with your partner since it opens the door for communication and discussion about the movie and sexual thoughts in general, and may very likely lead to your own brand of movie review!

Chapter 9

He Said...

Romance your sex life by Random Acts of Enticement

Entice to Excite!

WHAT are random acts of enticement?

Random acts of enticement are unpredictable activities we can incorporate in our activities of daily living to enhance, seduce and entice our lover. They reignite and tempt! They arouse and stir emotions. Sometimes they can cause physical arousal excitement and re awakening! Excite each other!!

WHY?

We are a society of programmed behavior. We buy flowers on Mother's day, ties on Father's day and start standing in line at our favorite coffee shop at 6:00 am in anticipation of our first morning brew! Most of us drive to work on the same route, eat the same meal day after day at our favorite restaurants. Our lives are routine, unimaginative and sometimes tiresome. Sex is no different. RUTS do happen! Predictability is a buzz kill. Random excitement causes our hormones to surge and soar creating erotic pleasure and exhilaration.

Try to be sensually unpredictable to entice and excite!

HOW?

Enticing or the art of seducing your partner may take some preplanning or it may even be spontaneous. Use your imagination. There are no pre-set rules. No defined times.

For some it may seem preplanned or forced, maybe even uncomfortable. Try to step out of your comfort zone but push through that uneasy feeling

WHEN?

Every day for the next 2 weeks each of try to practice at least one random acts of enticement. Random! No preset set amount of activities, no preplanned time. Be unpredictable! Vary the exercise! Use your sensual creativity! Inspire originality! Fan the smoldering embers to ignite passion and vitality.

Here are some suggested exercises:

Plan a romantic dinner with his/her favorite foods

Place a love note in his or her briefcase

Try Sexting a provocative proposal

Send him or her an erotic selfie

Go out for a surprise ice cream sundae

Slow dance in the living room. Naked?

Wake up to sweet nothings being whispered in your lover's ear

Spend some time at the local card store and stock up on cards to send to your lover. Send one this week!

Buy your partner a book they have been wanting to read- write a personal message in it!

Spray your perfume or cologne on a sheet of paper and write a love poem- place it in his or her lunch bag

Hide a pair of boxers, briefs in her purse!

Sneak a pair of panties in his inner suit pocket for him to discover all on his own!

Plan a bubble bath decked out with chocolate covered strawberries, romantic music and a favorite bottle of wine or champagne.

Use your creative imagination to ignite the flame that is smoldering to create a raging inferno!

Chapter 10

He Said...

Sex begins in the Kitchen: The Art of Sharing and Caring

WHAT?

Sharing and caring can enhance a relationship by reinforcing the bonds that originally connected you to each other. Remember the fun of dating? The anticipation of spending time together in a non-sexual way. It was exciting and enjoyable to spend some quality time together- Just being together. In our busy day-to-day activities we often forget to slow down and enjoy our partner's presence. Be present with our partners in the same physical space can be reminiscent of our earlier relationship when it was not overwhelmed with the demands of life.

Spend time together to enhance your feelings of connectedness- reengage and get reacquainted with each other. Adult alone time is important and vital to keep a sex life blossoming!

WHY?

Physical intimacy means spending time together- not only in a sexual erotic situation but also sometimes in a clothed activity! Being in each other's presence, just doing and enjoying each other's company can enhance your chemical and physical bond that you share.

Many of us have time to go to the gym for our daily workout or check hundreds of emails but often at the expense of our relationship! We often get distracted with work, chores, and social responsibilities not to mention children and the demands that they take us away from our lover! Reschedule your day together. Sometimes it is important to disconnect with the outside world and reconnect with your lover- just the 2 of you!

Remember what it was like?

HOW?

Over the course of the next 2 weeks, plan some adult alone time. Only the 2 of you- together! Maybe you will need to have a baby sitter or plan an activity when the kids are asleep or at their grandparents. Some advanced planning may be needed.

There are many activities you can do to without distant travel or breaking the bank! Use your imagination and creativity to enhance your alone time together. Try to do a new hobby together. Spend some time in each other's world. Go to the ballet even if you don't like it (Go Just... because ...she loves it!!) or watch that sporting event (Just because he acts like a silly fool with every touchdown!)

ENJOY spending time together! That's the goal. Perhaps try a museum visit, bike riding or go gallery hoping. Maybe do a puzzle. The Tango lessons you have been dreamed about? Spend time sharing in each other's hobbies. Try a novel hobby you both may have been interested in trying- take that ballroom dancing class, go surfing or sailing. Try a cooking class together.   The goal is togetherness and physical closeness!

WHEN?

Here are some exercises in which you can join together in a non-sexual way and reconnect physically and spend time together in each other's world. Try for 20-30 minutes a week!

Go to the grocery store together and then plan and cook a fancy meal together

Take a leisurely stroll on the beach together.

Go visit your favorite museum.

Take a sensual dancing course.

Do a puzzle together.

Take the dog for a walk!

Play a card game or backgammon.

Share your favorite movie with each other.

Learn a new hobby together

Share a swing ride at the playground!

Plan a mid-day rendezvous for lunch or a snack

Meet for after dinner drinks or cocktails

Go to the gym together and work out!

Take yoga or Pilates together

Spending time together will bring you closer emotionally and physically.

Slow down, enjoy, touch and connect with quality time!

Chapter 11

She Said ...
Shift the Focus to the Sexual Journey or Outercourse

What?

It's not uncommon for couples, particularly those in long term relationships, to view sex as yet just another boring chore to check off the to do list; intercourse, check. mutual orgasm, check. This Wham Bam Thank you ma'am approach may be great for the occasional quickie, when time constraints or privacy concerns arise.

Consider this: it's not always or only about intercourse, but rather the amazing ride you might experience prior to arrival, what we call *"the outercourse journey."*

Why?

Foreplay increases arousal and lubrication for women. It enriches sexual prowess and tension for men! Sexual play, other than intercourse builds anticipation which can only enhance the main event. Modifying, expanding and altering the sexual repertoire, effectively destroys boredom in the bedroom and introduces an element of surprise and novelty. This journey takes you from boredom to bliss

How?

Sensual foreplay might include:

An erotic massage

A long lingering hot sensual shower with touch and caresses,

Mutual self stimulation or masturbation

Oral play

Anal play.

IMPORTANT: Take your time. Go Slow! Enjoy and Linger!

Do not give in to the urge for immediate gratification and immediate orgasm.

Let the anticipation for orgasm build.

Enjoy the journey.

When?

Start with one session per week! Plan and set the stage. Insure no potential interruptions. A lock on the bedroom door will put your mind at ease and free you from the distraction and fear of interruption by curious children or restless pets.

Silence the smart phone and power down the tv.

Music, candles and ambient lighting are bonuses.

A sensual shower or bath can be soothing, relaxing and incredibly erotic. Take turns washing and exploring each other.

Enjoy soft touch sensual massage and discover erogenous zones you never knew existed. In fact, the skin is the largest organ in the body leaving plenty to explore.

Use a light and *subtly* scented massage oil. Lavender is soothing and relaxing.

Lemon, lavender and tea tree essential oils are also popular. Alternate giving and receiving.

Engage in oral pleasure as a change of pace. Experiment with anal play if you are bold.

Focus on the experience of sexual pleasure first; intercourse and mutual orgasm will likely follow and will be well worth the wait.

Chapter 12

She Said...

Positional Passion : Experiment with Sexual Position

WHAT?

It should come as no surprise that the most common position for vagina- penis intercourse is, you guessed it, missionary! Getting creative with sex positions might include thinking outside the box? Side to side? Rear entry? Doggie style? Maybe break with tradition and take sex out of the bedroom and into the shower, kitchen counter, staircase or SUV to name a few... no Cirque-du-Soleil flexibility required..... well maybe a little.

WHY?

Mixing it up and leaving your missionary comfort zone has many advantages.

First, it's fun! Experimenting with positioning introduces novelty, especially for long standing couples who have become accustomed to the hum drum Saturday night special... 11pm, after late night TV, missionary sex, then sleep. Consider this! Alternate positioning not only spices up the recipe, it may be the secret sauce you have been searching for in the bedroom bliss that can intensify intimacy. Try it, you may like it. You never know! As an added bonus, position change may also remedy some all too common ailments faced during sex play. Dryness and painful intercourse- side to side or female superior may be helpful. Female superior or straddling the lying down man may also be helpful for the man who may lose his erections quickly!

HOW?

You don't have to be super flexible or wildly adventurous to engage. Here are some old faithfuls.

Standing up is ideal for hitting your G-spot or taking it from the bedroom to the shower. Brace yourselves!

Spooning allows for relaxation and slower lovemaking and is a great early morning option; no morning breath worries, really!

Rear entry allows for deeper penetration... Bed optional!

Sitting face to face promises more intense eye to eye contact and intense connection... women love this stuff! Use of props like chairs and pillows may also help!

WHEN?

Try a new position each week for the next 4 weeks. See what you like and what is enjoyable.

Doggie style allows for comfortable and safe female positioning during late pregnancy. There is less pressure from a large uterus on the big blood vessels that are anatomically behind the uterus, for you third trimester daredevils.

Side by side with male spooning female is especially comfortable for those with low back pain.

Ride 'em cowboy is a wonderful option for women who are dealing with the super duper extra endowed male partner since depth of penetration and thrusting is on her terms. An added bonus? Extra clitoral stimulation for those in need and the anti is upped for vaginal orgasm. Go for it!

Maybe create your own special unique position!

.

Chapter 13

She Said...

Take Vacation Sex Home—Enjoy a Staycation!

WHAT?

A Staycation is a vacation spent at your own home rediscovering and enjoying your "castle" with your partner, while leaving daily responsibilities and stresses behind. This can be structured with a planned itinerary finding adventure around your own town or more relaxed by simply take advantage of a few days of rest and relaxation to decompress and reconnect intimately. Either way, as long as you vow not to catch up on work or allow laundry, bills or household chores to encroach on your vacation, a staycation can be truly relaxing, romantic and memorable.

WHY?

A stay at home vacation saves money, eliminates the exhaustion of travel, and can planned on your terms. Let's not forget the smelly disgusting arm rest wrestlers on the plane! After all, we all need a reprieve from the day to day monotony and stress of work and chores. Take personal time for more important pieces of life... such as intimacy and sex.

HOW?

Make it all-inclusive!

Turn your home into a boutique hotel

- Make up the bed like hotels do with new crisp, white linens and a neatly folded inviting duvet, with lots of pillows
- Ditch your sweats and upgrade to plush white terry robes and silky sexy lingerie. Silk boxers for him too!
- Stock the bathroom with a super sumptuous body wash for romantic showers or baths together.
- Fresh flowers help create a sensual mood too!
- Create a mini-bar with seductive snacks like chocolate covered fruit, nuts and champagne
- Order room service with your favorite take-out menus, fancy trays and champagne flutes for a "brunch in bed" bonus!
- Watch movies in bed; cue up a Netflix lineup in advance
- Put chocolates on your pillow; splurge on decadent treats you wouldn't usually buy

Act like tourists in your hometown

- Plan a daily itinerary
- Visit a local museum or gallery

- Incorporate fitness with a fun bike ride or hike; tennis anyone? Try a spin or yoga class together
- Go to a wine bar or have outdoor afternoon cocktails. Explore a new eatery!
- Cook romantic meals together or dine out if you prefer; try new exotic foods
- Go shopping together
- Schedule a couples massage or spa treatments. They even can be ordered right to your door!
- Cuddle by the fire even if it is summer time and sweltering!
- Take in a movie, show or sporting event
- Take a nap together- NUDE?
- Curl up together with a good book on a chair for 2 or loveseat
- Play board games

Unplugging is mandatory

- Insure your phone goes immediately to voicemail
- Set email autoreply to "out of office"
- Put your phone on airplane mode!
- Send children and pets on their own vacation with grandparents or friends
- Turn off alarm clocks … its ok to sleep in!

WHEN?

Anytime! That's the beauty of a staycation!

"Vacation Sex" can be found right in your own back yard....
Literally.

No packing.

No airports

No TSA or security lines.

No pushing or shoving storing overhead luggage.

No airfare

No hotel!

No rental car!

Yes to Fun

BON VOYAGE!

Chapter 14
He Said...
Building Staying Power

What is building Staying Power!

For both men and women pushing yourself to the peak of sexual pleasure, often called "Edging" can heighten sexual pleasure and believe it or not- for some men even result in a multi orgasmic experience. This technique of edging is often the focus of tantric sexual pleasure! Enjoying sexual stimulation and excitement without ejaculation or orgasm becomes the new goal! For men, they can gain sexual control by uncoupling erection and ejaculation. He can be aroused, experience euphoria and pleasure and return to a still and quiet baseline, only to return to sexual dynamism minutes later. Women too, can experience sexual euphoria with or without orgasmic experience.

How do you Develop Staying Power.

Improving sexual staying power may take some hard work and effort. It may even take several attempts to help heighten your pleasure and reach your point of ejaculatory release (the exact point right before you will orgasm) or signals for orgasmic intensity. There are some exercises that can help both a man or woman gain more control over his or her pelvic floor.

First try to contract your pelvic muscles- these are the muscles that you use when you are urinating. Try to stop your urine flow mid-stream. Hold this pose for several seconds, then release, then repeat multiple times. In essence, you are exercising the pelvis. Doing Kegel exercises for both men and women can help strengthen the pelvic floor. Try doing this exercise several times a day and in repeats of 10 squeeze then release. Start off with one repetition per day and work your way up to increased reps.

For women, try getting aroused and stimulated- focus on the exact time before orgasm. Once you feel that you are approaching the orgasmic release- stop stimulation! Breathe and be calm! Relax! Don't touch or be touched! Do some deep breathing and relax! One you have returned to a more unaroused baseline, start again with some mild sexual stimulation. You can repeat this process several times- until you and your partner want to experience mind blowing multi-orgasmic release!

Another exercises is called the "Squeeze Stop technique". Once a man is stimulated with an erection, and he is approaching the point of ejaculatory release, his partner or he may squeeze the frenulum (or area below the tip of the penis) and try to breathe and relax. Breathe, Relax and stay focused! In essence you are uncoupling the erection response with orgasm or ejaculation. Do not be discouraged if it takes some time and practice to help control when you finally progress to orgasm! It's not uncommon to ejaculate when you think you have stopped! Practice makes perfect!

Why would I want to experience Increased Sexual Prowess?

Uncoupling orgasm and erection or sexual arousal can prolong and intensify the sexual experience. Couples will tend to focus on the sexual journey rather than sex or orgasm as a goal oriented event.

For many couples, sex is like a sporting event, the goal of a hard penis in a wet or ready vagina must be achieved within a certain time frame with successful intercourse for the experience to be satisfying and pleasurable.

Sometimes in men who have a short refractory period (the restful bliss between erections) ejaculations may be able to experience multiple orgasmic responses in rapid succession. Remember the older you get the longer your refractory period typically becomes! Young men can often have sex multiple times a day whereas older gents it may be 1 time every few days. Even so, don't give up! Many men can learn and can experience multiple orgasms too! Practice strengthening your pelvic floor!

Uncoupling arousal with orgasm takes the pressure of performance. The couple can focus on the journey of sexual pleasure without a goal in mind! They can prolong the sexual voyage by heightening sensuality, happiness and strengthening intimacy. There is nothing wrong with a quickie, yes we agree, but sometimes a prolonged session of hot sweaty lovemaking will do the trick!

When to do the exercises?
Sometime this week, each of you should try to edge or push yourself to the limit of orgasmic response but then stop. Stop short of orgasm. Calm back down, and try to edge yourself to the delight of sexual pleasure. Try this experience alone first; maybe in the shower or bath. Then do it together.

Allow yourself to orgasm if you want. There is no judgment or number of times you could, should or must bring yourself or your partner to the peak of sexual bliss before your final indulgence.

Enjoy the process not the goal.

Chapter 15

He Said ...

Food glorious food!   and Edible Erotic Sexuality

What do Sex and Food have to do with each other?

We are all foodies!   We love our morning nonfat caramel macchiato coffee or our fettuccini Alfredo with extra cream sauce.   Food preparation is often the shared guarded time when a couple can be together in the kitchen preparing a meal to share. As the best seller, *Sex begins in the Kitchen* or Dr. Murray Friedman's book, Sex *is like a Peanut Butter Sandwich* often reiterate, sex and food are often intertwined!   Food preparation time can be a sensual time, sharing and enjoying .. not to mention a time where families can catching up on the days' events.

Food can also be an erotic and sensual experience when shared together in an intimate setting. It's not all champagne and whipped cream.... Or honey and chocolate... Consider using your appetite and imagination.

WHY?

Since recorded history civilization has been searching for the secret to sexual satisfaction. Nearly every ancient empire searched for the fountain of sexual vitality- the benefit of a selected herb, food, or supplemental product for sexual enhancement, satisfaction, or desire.

Food has always been considered an aphrodisiac.

What is an aphrodisiac? Technically, it is a substance which arouses or intensifies sexual pleasure, sexual desire or performance. Believe it or not, the perception that food can enhance sex has been around for centuries and some cultures even advocate eating some strange and bizarre foods to enhance sexual vitality! One culture advocated eating an animal's testicles to enhance sexual expertise. Secret properties, or nutrients texture may directly or indirectly enhance sexual performance. Some people get turned on by food that may look like genitals: male phallic Identity or the penis and testicles has been linked to Avocados (which hang from tree in pairs) or long vegetables like the Asparagus, Carrots, Celery, Rhino horn and of course the common banana.

Who has not practiced oral sex on a banana? For women, some other foods are sensual like Dates, Figs, Eggs, Garlic, pomegranate, oysters and artichoke. Don't ask us ... but it's all documented in the history books. It either for their appearance or their nutrients!

Being overweight or obese can certainly negatively impact your sexual response and sexual satisfaction! We are not sure if it is directly impacts sexual hormones or neurotransmitters or if obesity interferes with other factors like changes in self-esteem. Most likely, it's a combination of multiple factors.

The verdict is definitely out! Being your correct weight for height certainly can recharge your sexual battery. A Mediterranean Diet (one that is rich in fruits, vegetables, whole grains, legumes, nuts (especially walnuts) and olive oil, and very low on the red meat, refined grains, and processed foods) has been scientifically proven to be cardio protective, enhance overall general health and wellness and also has been studied to show that it improves sexuality.

The Truth about Chocolate:
Chocolate, which the Aztecs referred to as the "nourishment of the Gods" is the most popular food associated with sexuality. Apparently history books claim that Montezuma drank 50 goblets of chocolate per day to enhance his sexual drive and to avoid sexual exhaustion.

Chocolate was also used as currency; 10 beans could buy a rabbit, 12 could a courtesan.

Sounds untrue but there are men and women who appear to be susceptible to the serotonin response that chocolate gives within the brain. Yes, they really become chocoholics. They are chocolate junkies!

Yes Honey! Origin of the word Honeymoon!
Newlyweds supposedly consumed honey wine to increase sexual stamina- especially on that special night after the wedding! No science to back it up but it is a romantic folktale!

HOW?
Start by planning a special erotic meal together! Focus on all the details. Make your shopping list of lustful items!

Plan the menu carefully and focus on yummy food choices!

Pick sensual foods that are exciting to touch, scent and visually appealing

Pick a Seductive Menu:
        Limit wine or Champagne
                Be careful as Macbeth once said:

> "What three things does drink especially
> provoke… lechery, sir, it provokes, and
> unprovoked; it provokes the desire but it
> takes away performance "

Include some velvety Chocolate

A brief word on Food Fetishism

In the spirit of the popular movie, 9½ weeks, try to incorporate food into your sex play. Remember Samantha in the popular television show "Sex and the City" adorning her naked body with homemade sushi for her lover on Valentine's Day. Pick something you both enjoy and dare to explore and play with your food! Edible sexual play may satisfy both your hunger for fun wild sex and a grumbling stomach!

WHEN?

Over the course of the next 2 weeks each of you should plan one special meal.

Pay particular attention the menu. Maybe it is time to dust off that favorite recipe of your spouse and break the bank for the loved caviar?

Plan the entire delectable feast from start all the way down to dessert!

Plan the meal with some elements of secrecy. Maybe divide up the courses and don't share what each of you are preparing! Consider only sharing the menu on the day of the feast.

Make enough time for food preparation and enjoy your time together preparing the culinary journey. After dinner, consider bringing something special and edible into the bedroom!

Be certain to set the stage for a night of erotic pleasure. No interruptions, privacy, lighting, scented candles and soft music may all enhance the food fiesta!

Try to be daring and incorporate some food into your sensual play. Maybe you want to start off slow with some whipped cream or honey? Or for the daring... maybe ice cream or ice cubes in your mouth as you perform oral pleasure. Use your imagination to unleash your hidden food fetish!

Chapter 16

She Said...

Enjoy Liquid Lovemaking:

The World of Moisturizers and Lubricants

WHAT is liquid lovemaking?

Whether it is to prevent or treat vaginal dryness or better yet to enhance the sexual experience, there are a multitude lotions, notions and potions available to bring a "juicier" experience to the bedroom. Mositurizers maintain the vagina, lubricants are for lovemaking! A great combo choice is a vaginal hybrid! These combine both a vaginal moisturizer and lubricant in one! Two popular hybrids are Luvena and Lubrigyn cream. They, are for regular use to prevent and treat vaginal dryness. They may be used 2 times a week to maintain the ridges and folds within the vagina. Both of these products contain no hormones. Luvena maybe be actually help prevent recurrent vaginal infections. Lubrigyn cream, is an almond oil based product that is made in Italy has both elastin and sodium hyluronate. You still should consider a lubricant during sex.

Lubricants galore, abound the shelves for on demand use during sexual play, be it vaginal, oral or anal pleasure. Massage oils enhance even the gentlest touch especially when an essential oil is in the mix. Liquid enhancers, like Zestra (feminine arousal oil) or 007 or 099 sexcellence creams , can add an extra zip, when applied to the clitoris prior to sex play, if you dare!

WHY?

Some women will experience pain during sex particularly during menopause when estrogen levels drop significantly. Women on the birth control pill or those breastfeeding or with chronic diseases such as diabetes, sjogren's disease or cancer may find intercourse uncomfortably irritating and painful. A regimen of regular moisturizers and on demand lubricants will surely help to regain and retain vaginal moisture and keep sex pleasurable rather than painful.

Lubricants can heighten sexual pleasure. In fact, the very act of applying lubricant in front of or to your partner is sensual. Penetration is facilitated and sensation heightened. Many couples actually use lubricant to enhance and intensify the sexual experience! You do not need to be dry- you may want to enhance and spice up a "dry" sex life.

HOW?

Shop in store or on-line (MiddlesexMD.com is our favorite) with or without your partner.

You will find water based, silicone (really slick) , oil based, flavored, warming and cooling lubricants and a variety of massage oils. Coconut oil or scented and flavored options are very popular. Remember things often found around the house that are petroleum based, (for exemple mineral oil or vaseline) are better left in your medicine cabinet and not in your privates! (bacterial infections have been reported!)

Sexual lubricants can be applied liberally to the vaginal opening, on the vulva and the penis. Try diferent kinds and experiment by incorporating them into sexual play if you like.

WHEN?

Ladies, plan on making a vaginal moisturizer part of your regular routine, just like using face or skin cream. Consider an over the counter or a compounded hyaluronic acid blend such as Sexcellence cream, once or twice weekly for wonderful and lasting vaginal moisture and elasticity. Sexcellence cream is a special propirietary mositurizer- it can be inserted day or night and is not meant for intercourse, but rather for regularly scheduled use. (See appendix for prescribing instructions)

For some women, a local vaginal estrogen might also be prescribed in addition or in place of this.

For clitoral or sexual enhancers....

The secret weapon try Sexcellence 007-

This enhancer will transform the mundane experience into a James Bond-esque romp in the hay.

The top espionage secret Agent: Sexcellence 099

Only for the daring and adventurous... Do you think you can handle it!!

Keep your favorite lubricant on hand and readily available for sexual play. We recommend using an attractive and discreet bedside bottle or keeping it nearby in a night-table drawer for spontaneity. Make it part of the sex scene!

Unless you are sensitive, take advantage of the abundance of available lubricants and mix it up.

Flavored lubricants add spice to oral pleasure.

Cooling or warming lubricants can be super sexy.

The options are endless.

Surprise your partner with a novel lubricant or massage oil on date night.

Consider enhancers for special occasions or better yet as a "random act of kindness."

Add excitement to shower sex with a silicone super slick longer lasting lubricant.... brace yourself! (Remember you dont want to be the next episode of sex brought me to the emergency room... silicone lubes on the shower floor can be Slippery... proceed with caution!!!)

Chapter 17

She Said...

Let's talk a Walk on the Wild Side

WHAT?

Look around. We are creatures of habit. We all drive to work the same way, drink the same type of coffee and go to our favorite restaurants while ordering the same meal. Sex is no different. It can become predictable and routine. The Saturday night special. We come to predict and expect a certain sexual script. Sometimes taking a hot shower then putting on his lucky boxer shorts and turning off the late night television may be the indicator that romance is about to percolate.

When we are predictable with sex a couple can become entrenched boredom. You are at risk for quick foreplay, short arousal and sex can become dry. Taking a walk on the wild side in the bedroom might include a wide range of activities with varying degrees of risk, taboo and seduction. From a simple game of strip poker, to joining the mile high club to threesomes or porn, to BDSM (bondage and discipline, sadism and masochism) it really is anything goes. While this may not be for the faint of heart, make no mistake, men and women from all walks of life, all ages, religious backgrounds and religions – ALL indulge.

Why is sexual excitement important?

Sexual excitement and novelty can change your hormones! Dopamine and norepinephrine are both increased with sexual dynamism which not only enhance the sexual response but can also lead to increased feelings of closeness. Novelty not only helps build the excitement between the couple but can improve the biological connection between the couple

Seemingly naughty behavior in the bedroom introduces not only novelty but heightens excitement. The forbidden... is a SERIOUS turn on for many. Fantasy takes you deep into another character and frees you from the restriction of "real life." You can pretend and play real live adult make believe.

HOW?

Increasing excitement into a relationship can take many forms- from the very simple intervention like change the time of the day you are intimate to the more daring. Using sexual accessories made for him and her can also provide new opportunities for Sexploration and excitement.

Leave your inhibitions and judgment behind and have an open dialogue and communicate with each other about your sexual desires, turn offs. Set the ground rules and clearly define the boundaries.

There really is no right or wrong between consenting adults.

The possibilities are endless.

WHEN?

Over the next 2 weeks think about how and when you can bring some novelty into your sex life.

Lets start with baby steps.

Time of the day sex change
If you are a nighttime sex person, wake up early to enjoy a romp in the hay.

Consider a sexual relocation program.
The majority of couples have sex ONLY in a bed and ONLY in the master bedroom. For added excitement, try another room in the house, discreetly in the back of your SUV (maybe start with it parked in the garage then be adventorous any play in

the driveway, or even consider joining the mile high club. Sex in the shower can also be steamy and FUN!

Challenge your partner to a hot game of strip poker or truth or dare. Loser is left with no clothes on?..... Sounds more like a win win! Try a sexual vibrator! Both men and women can enjoy the exploration with a sexual device. Some favorites include the high end Lelo brand (lelo.com). Another favorite is the FIERA which is an "Arouser for Her" which is designed to be worn before sex to help her mind and body feel more in the mood

Visit a virtual novelty store, (a favorite web site that provides discrete sexual accessory purchase and delivery is MiddlesexMD) or real adult sex shop. There's a reason sexual accessories are a multi-billion dollar business. Include some props during sex play such as blindfolds, feather ticklers, nipple clamps, or silk ties as handcuffs. What about the riding crop you have been craving!

Do not forget erotic clothing too!

Feeling WILDER... Take a walk on the wilder side? Maybe BDSM (read next chapter too) is your bag... or to try it at least...

While this "sexercise" may not be your cup of tea, if you are going to indulge, above all, safety first.

Try something wild and new in your next sexual experience!

Chapter 18

He Said...

Some People like Lima Beans

Ever Wonder about BDSM? Does your sex life need a little Dose of 50 shades of Grey?

What is BDSM?

What exactly is BDSM? Intrigued by the concept of power play exchanges? BDSM actually stands for Bondage, Discipline, Sadism and Masochism. It is commonly known as an exchange of sexual power of dominance and submission between two consenting partners. It may also involve props and or sexual toys, from the vanilla items like feathers or blindfolds to the more hardcore whips, chains, clamps and masks.

Some couples enjoy giving or receiving pain to each other. Other may actively flog or whip the other each during their role-playing sexual activities.

"Some people like lima beans when others don't enjoy them in their salad or meals." Everyone has different sexual tastes and needs!

While it may or may not be for you and your partner, it's important to chat about the possibilities and the activities you may want to investigate.

Some people will enjoy the fantasy to change their typical roles during sex- this variation may have heighten sexual excitement, and improve sensual awareness. It can also effect on your neurohormones by increasing endorphin or oxytocin release!

Some may even crave the experience of escape. The fantasy of escapism from their normal day to day may add some carnal thrills to an otherwise dull sex life. Consider the high-powered business executive who is constantly making important financial decisions who may want to be submissive and spanked by a sassy bossy mean dominatrix and let the decisions be made for him; he may enjoy being dominated.

The mousy mailroom clerk who is always the brunt of people's criticisms may desire to be in control and bossy- controlling her sexual pleasure and her sexual play!

Why incorporate BDSM?
We all have roles in our relationships. Sometimes one is more versed at balancing the checkbook while others enjoy cooking or cleaning. These roles often develop over time and

sometimes get set in stone. Within most relationships there is a differential of power, a dominant forceful personality and a one who maybe more submissive. Sometime we get accustomed to the roles we experience and other times we get bored or frustrated within our own self-defined expectations.

These roles we play in the relationship game of power are also often seen in the bedroom. Sexually, someone initiates and someone is more receptive!

One may be more aggressive and the other more playful and docile. In a sensual relationship exploring your roles may add dynamism to a humdrum sex life. Pushing you and your partner to either solidify your roles or be daring enough to experience the side you have never explored. It may be exciting and pleasurable- fearful yet rewarding. Opening yourself and your sexual repertoire to new experiences such as BDSM may heighten your arousal and lead to personal growth and awareness.

You may discover new sexual pleasures with your partner!

How to incorporate BDSM into sex play?

BDSM means a variety of things to different people. To some it is a power exchange or the eroticization of either physical or emotional pain. For others it means role-playing during sex from scenarios like Slap & Tickle me to Stand & Model. There are many themes for BDSM sexual play, which can include any activities such as bondage (ropes and tying each other up) to spanking and role-playing. Some couples may go to extremes and incorporate pain and humiliation. Remember that this is only fantasy and discuss your limits and expectations with your partner.

When to try BDSM?

Over the next week sit and discuss the concepts of power play with your partner. Maybe buy a copy of 50 Shades of Gray or if you have one read over selected chapters that you thought were interesting.

You may want to go slow and perhaps just start with a feather and tickle your partner as he or she remains still and instructed not to move or respond.

First, set some ground rules. Since practices might transform the erotic into the painful, be sure to establish a safe word which under all circumstances, ceases play immediately. This rule is never broken... EVER! Some stop words include.... RED, STOP, cupcake or broccoli (yes we have heard it all). Be creative and choose something meaningful to you both!

Maybe your adventurous side has kicked in and you can consider some light bondage with some loose knots or handcuffs and maybe a blindfold.

Common dominant versus submissive themes include

Guard and Prisioner
Master and Slave
Teacher and Bad student
Coach and Athlete

Prepare! Costumes and props are mandatory.

Others may like acting out specific scenarios.... some sexual role playing may tantilize

Some fantasy common themes include

The Pizza Delivery Man
Pretend you have falsely ordered a pizza to get the hot delivery man into your house!

The Fireman Rescue

You inadventently call 911 (pretend of course) for a cat rescue which is trapped in your tree to draw the sexy fireman with a huge hose to your door

The Anonymous Pick Up

You both go out on date but are pretending that you dont even know each other. Try to pcik up each other and score a pseudo one night stand

The French Maid/ Butler

Dress up as a maid or butler and provide extra special attention to the hotel guest as you have barged in unexpectedly to help tidy up the hotel room.

There are even places you can explore in a variety of cities that have rooms decorated as formal sets (the doctors office, the prison ward, the airplane first class) where you can explore in private. Some even offer special props and the opportunity for private filmings so you can imortalize your sexual fantasy

Let your imagination be your compass, and the trust and discussions with your partner your guidebook.

Chapter 19

He Said...

Make Sex Spicy with a Relationship Fantasy Box

What?

Creating a box of sensual excitement by the fantasy Box!

Creating a fantasy box can be an adventure in and of itself. Plan an afternoon or evening to the local craft store and buy a wooden box to decorate or just dust off an old shoe box.

Decorate it with memories of your relationship- photos, keepsakes or other trinkets that remind you both. No photos of kids! Keep it all about your relationship! Store it an adult secret place. No children allowed. Your box is now ready to be filled!

How do I fill the fantasy box?

Fantasies... YIKES... I have no idea

Next step towards completing the fantasy box is when each of you takes some time in private to think of 3 sexual and 3 non-sexual fantasies, each.

That makes 12 fantasies- six sexual and six non sexual.

Don't forget to discuss your limits with your partner.

Maybe you always wanted to visit that new museum downtown, or that 5 star restaurant but life always got in the way of your plan. Maybe it is a mini trip to a local nudist resort? Maybe you're more adventurous and want to roleplay with costumes and scenarios.

Dust off your imagination; leave your inhibitions behind.

Even the most vivacious couples need some help! Here are common sexual fantasies...

*Play with props- buy a new vibrator and use it on each other.

*Dress up and pretend!

* The feather duster can be erotic and sexy

*Water and Sex play often Mix!

     Sex in the shower!

     Sex in the Bath!

     Sex in the hot tub!

     Sex In the swimming pool.

*Sex in the Sauna can be hot sweaty fun!

* Sexual positions
  - try something new and exciting
  - Maybe a new location- how about sex in the kitchen

Consider your partner and what they would like too!

A word of sexual caution: If bringing outside members into your sexual play such as inviting a third to join in, or a ménage a trois is not in you or your partner's sexual comfort zone- it shouldn't be included. Maybe discuss some of these issues beforehand to avoid mixed messages and being threatened to be outside of your comfort zone!

Be mindful of your values and level of comfort.

Be honest and open with your partner.

Next step is to write down each fantasy on separate piece of paper and fold it up.

Place the folded pieces of paper in the box!

Now your fantasy box is ready!

WHY?

We are all creatures of habit! We love routine from our morning coffee to our drive to work. Predictability brings comfort. Sometimes novelty is new and exciting! It stimulates our neurotransmitters or brain chemicals to get revved up and creates euphoria and excitement. With novelty also comes the release of the cuddle hormone oxytocin! Novelty and new sexual and non-sexual experiences shared with a couple can enhance and strengthen the intimacy in a relationship.

WHEN?

Spice up your sex life with some fantasy play. This week, you and your spouse decorate a box together. Create the fantasy box as described above.

Commit to one fantasy each month.

Take turns choosing to execute the fantasy!

You should be alternating between you and your partner. Keep the fantasy play secret.

The planner should plan the entire fantasy from start to finish, only altering his or her partner on the day of the event. Try to build the anticipation.

Send a sensual text message or leave a well-placed love note-reminding that its fantasy day! Let's the sensuality smolder and brew!

Chapter 20

She said...

Get Professional Counseling and Therapy

WHAT?

Sex therapy delves into the biological, psychological and interpersonal aspects of sexual expression in an intense way. The focus of sex therapy treatment is to give permission to a couple or individual to enjoy sex and to help resolve conflicts and alleviate anxiety as it relates to intimacy.

WHY?

Just because you're seeking help doesn't mean your relationship is in trouble. It may only need a little fine sexual tune up.

Counselors and sex therapists are there to help set realistic expectations and help guide you and your partner to a more satisfying and sexual union. They start by educating couples and individuals about anatomy, physiology and the sexual response cycle. The stages of sexual response made famous by Masters and Johnson, excitement, plateau, orgasm and resolution, are typically reviewed while keeping in mind that women's sexual functioning is complex, and intimacy and relationship satisfaction are tantamount.

HOW?

Typical counseling interventions include cognitive behavioral therapy (CBT) (how can we use behaviors or actions to change thinking! Homework exercises like the ones in this book are often prescribed), intensive sex therapy (may involve psychotherapy and/or.... Freud and perhaps childhood memories and or traumas), and the Buddhist tradition of mindfulness training.

CBT employs behavioral therapy focusing on modifying thoughts and beliefs that interfere with intimacy and sexual enjoyment..

Mindfulness encourages "being in the moment" and a focus on the here and now, rather than worrying about the "what if's of future" or issues past.

Sex therapists may assign homework with structured erotic experiences to be carried out in the privacy of the home on your terms.

WHEN?

Men and women should be empowered and encouraged to take charge of their sexual health. Both sexes who do not respond to medical intervention or simple office based counseling often could benefit from more structured brief intervention of counseling or in depth therapy.

Misinformation about sexual norms is often misrepresented by the media. Sexual Myths are rampant and should be corrected and health care professionals.

HOW?

Make an appointment today for yourself or for you and your partner. Check out the therapist online and look at credentials. Make some phone calls and see if the counselor or therapist is willing to discuss their mode of treatment beforehand.

Making an appointment and following through with the visit DOES NOT mean there is a serious relationship issue or that you're headed to divorce. What it does mean is that you have recognized that there is an issue that should and could be addressed! Seize control and take back the power of your sexual destiny. Getting help is often the first step forward!

Getting Help

Where can I seek help for you and your partner?

There are many health care providers who claim to be sexual experts so choosing the correct health care professional for your specific complaint is always important. Medical doctors like gynecologists or urologists sometimes have a special interest in sexual medicine mental health care professionals like psychologists, social workers or psychiatrists, can also be helpful in treating sexual problems. Be certain to verify credentials as qualifications and categories often change from state to state and location to location. The doctors who have chosen to specialize in sexual medicine often are more compassionate, and empathic. Sex therapists are mental health care providers who have specialized training in the diagnosis and treatment of sexual complaints.

Contact the American Association of Sex Educators, Therapists and Counselors (AASECT www.aasect.org)) for trained therapists or counselors in your neighborhood. Check the credentials of the specialist you plan to see and verify if they take insurance. Sometimes local clergy or other religious leaders can also help with faith based sexual counseling!

Perhaps most importantly is do not be afraid to seek medical professional help, there are highly skilled sexual health care experts who understand that intimacy and connectedness is paramount to quality of life.

Have the courage to seek help and restore your sexuality and sensuality.

Some Final Words of Wisdom from the Sexcellent team
By the He said She said DUO...

Family, friends, success and health are lifelong goals for many but we often neglect our Lifelong goal of sexual vitality...

Life goals should Include Lifelong Sexual Vitality.
Here is a recipe for success...

Lifelong sexual wellness is a commitment to yourself, your partner and your relationship. Boredom is always a threat. Try to keep doing new and exciting things with your partner- not only does it influence hormones and neurotransmitters that can enhance intimacy and relationship but it can lead to decreased sexual boredom.

Novelty triggers the transmitter dopamine to be released from the brain, which can stimulate feelings of connectedness and attraction. It can enhance bonding. Ride a rollercoaster, dance naked in the living room and use your creativity and imagination. Novel experiences that are shared together as a committed couple can increase closeness and sensual and sexual feelings. It develops the bonds that will solidify your relationship.

Include these tips to promote sexual health and general health and wellness too

Everyone knows these....
 Eat all the right foods
 Get a lot of sleep
 Maintain and active aerobic exercise plan
 Decrease your stress

Apparently there's more to "good health" than physical activity and good nutrition. Here are a few ways to boost your health and your long-term sexual satisfaction.

• Maintain your social and community ties
Numerous studies have linked social support to improved immune function, longevity, a lower risk of heart disease, and speedier recovery from serious illness and surgery. Research shows that socially active individuals were just as healthy as their counterparts who exercised regularly, and that social engagement was more important than blood pressure and cholesterol levels in determining longevity. These connections should be genuine: Casual acquaintances and cocktail party chatter are no substitutes for fast friends and abiding relationships.

• Get a pet

The Centers for Disease Control and Prevention reports that having a pet can lower your blood pressure decrease levels of cholesterol and triglycerides, and moderate feelings of loneliness. Studies show that cats and dogs reduced blood pressure and heart rate in a group of high-stress stockbrokers.

•Slow down... Relax and Take a vacation

Research demonstrates that women who took a vacation only once in two years had a higher risk of depression and stress than those who took two or more vacations a year. They were also more likely to report lower marital satisfaction.

Vacations are good for the heart—both for men and women. Women who take two or more vacations a year have half the risk of developing coronary heart disease or other serious heart problems.

• Laugh out loud. A big belly laugh...

In Anatomy of an Illness, famed magazine editor Norman Cousins wrote that ten minutes of belly laughter bought him two hours of painless sleep. Research at Loma Linda University in California has shown that laughter increases the number and activity level of the body's natural killer cells and reduces stress hormones that have been linked to heart disease.

- Pray or Meditate

Although scientific proof of the efficacy of prayer lags behind claims, a 2001 study in the British Medical Journal reports that saying the rosary (or repeating yoga mantras) may be good for the heart by synchronizing breathing with cardiovascular rhythms. Proponents of the health benefits of prayer say it improves coping mechanisms and produces better health outcomes. Numerous studies have reported multiple health benefits from meditation (particularly Transcendental Meditation), among them stress reduction, improved recovery from surgery, lower blood pressure, improved pain management, and a longer lifespan.

- Marriage or Lifetime Companion-

Being committed has been shown to reduce illnesses and increase longevity. Healthy sex lives have also increased longevity and decreased depression rates.

Guide to Sexual Resources to Reignite your Passion

Sexual Accessories

Lelo

Self-stimulators for him and her from the entry level to gold plated. A device for all budgets and occasions! www.lelo.com

Milli™ By Materna Medical

Milli is the only dilator that can expand after the device is already inserted which leads to less anxiety with insertion. Smaller dilation increments, 1 mm at a time, lead to more control and patients to push their progress. It also contains a 2-setting vibration option and a soft silicone cover. It is easy to use, stylishly designed, and charges using USB discretely in its case for easy storage. It is also easier to clean a single device than multiple dilators. For more information and purchasing details visit www.millimedical.com

Fiera

Fiera ® is a new personal care product that works with a woman's body to enhance sexual arousal and increase desire, naturally. The unique design, co-created with women and sexual health experts, uses a proprietary combination of suction and gentle stimulation that helps get you ready for an intimate and enjoyable sexual experience with your partner. Women also report that regular use of Fiera over a 4-week period increased their level of sexual desire so they're ready and excited when the moment is right.

Fiera helps encourage blood flow in the clitoris, a key physical reaction that signals your body that you're ready for sex. It is small, discreet, and hands-free but offers a huge punch for sexual vitality. Dr Krychman preformed the FAME trial (Fiera at Midlife Experience) clinical prospective case series, which was presented as a moderated poster at the Sexual Medicine Society North America Annual Meeting. This trial demonstrated the Fiera use independent of sexual intercourse enhanced sexual pleasure and satisfaction! More information about fiera at www.fiera.com.

Sinclair Institute

Sexual accessories and videos for anyone's delight and pleasure.

www.sinclairinstitute.com

Literotica.com

Erotic literature.

MiddlesexMD.com

MiddlesexMD.com is a resource begun by menopause care specialist Dr. Barb DePree when she couldn't find good products for her patients at places they'd be comfortable to frequent. The site began with extensive information helpful to couples who wanted to maintain their intimacy through perimenopause and menopause, including products chosen for efficacy and quality, available from the privacy of your home. Dr. Barb blogs regularly and publishes a podcast twice a month; whether you follow either or not, that means search results on the website are especially rich.

Moisturizers and Lubricants

Lubrigyn Lotion and Cream

Lubrigyn Lotion: is creamy lotion rather than a lather and works gently to cleanse and moisturize the delicate vulva area. It is for ongoing use since it's made with natural active ingredients, is pH balanced and hypoallergenic.

Lubrigyn Cream relieves vaginal dryness, provides long lasting lubrication (for internal use) and supplements natural moisture. It is recommended for sensitive skin.

Lubrigyn products are available at CVS pharmacy.

RepHresh Gel

RepHresh vaginal gel normalizes vaginal pH to the healthy 3.8-4.5 range to reduce the risk of common issues like itch, odor, and discomfort. The bio adhesive polymer, polycarbophil, bonds to the vagina's epithelial cells and restores a healthy pH for up to 3-days. By keeping the vaginal pH balanced, RepHresh reduces the risk of developing Bacterial Vaginosis (BV), and keeps bacteria that cause odor from overpopulating.

Replens Vaginal Moisturizer

Replens vaginal moisturizer is an estrogen-free, long-lasting vaginal moisturizer that provides immediate relief of vaginal dryness and replenishes moisture for up to 3-days. Replens' active ingredient, polycarbophil balances pH to normal and attaches to vaginal cells, but also delivers continuous moisture for women post-partum, in menopause or following a cancer treatment.

Replens Silky Smooth

Replens Silky Smooth is a silicone-based lubricant to make intercourse very slick and reduce the chances of abrasion to nil in most cases. Because it's silicone, it lasts longer than water based lubricants, its preservative free and compatible with natural rubber latex, poly-isoprene, and polyurethane condoms.

HYALO GYN®

Hyalogyn ® is a personal lubricant, for penile and/or vaginal application, intended to moisturize and lubricate, to enhance the ease and comfort of intimate sexual activity and supplement the body's natural lubrication. This product is compatible with condoms: lubricated/non-lubricated latex, lubricated polyurethane, lubricated natural skin.

Composition: The principal component: Hydeal-D® (hyaluronic acid derivative).

Other components: Propylene glycol, carbomer (Carbopol 974P), methyl p-hydroxybenzoate, propyl p-hydroxybenzoate, sodium hydroxide and purified water.

It can be purchased only online at www.hyalogyn.com

Pre-Seed

Pre-Seed is the only Food and Drug (FDA) cleared, clinically tested fertility friendly lubricant on the market that was developed specifically for couples who are trying to conceive. Pre-Seed is properly pH balanced and isotonic to mimic a woman's natural secretions and is sperm friendly. It is **safe to use during conception.** Pre-Seed is glycerin-free, allowing sperm to swim freely and is formulated with antioxidants to helps support sperm motility.

Good Clean Love

Good Clean Love is revolutionizing the sexual health product industry with organic solutions for intimacy and sexual health. As a women-owned, certified B corporation, Good Clean Love is dedicated to providing products made from organic/natural ingredients and free of petrochemicals, parabens and glycerin. Our water-based formulas are iso-osmotic and mimic the body's natural lubrication without all the harsh chemicals associated with conventional personal lubricants. Good Clean Love's lubricants are designed to work with the body because good sex isn't about side effects. Sold in over 20,000 retail locations, Good Clean Love is proud to be the top-selling organic intimacy brand on the market.

Uberlube: It's not just for SEX

Uberlube for Sex: Not just slippery, Uberlube transfers sensation while reducing friction. It feels silky and performs as long as you're using it. When Uberlube stops being manipulated, it starts to dissipate. Not harmful to healthy bacteria or pH levels. Physician recommended, used in OB-GYN practices. Scentless, tasteless and non-staining; not sticky, tacky or oily. Understated design for nightstand and out and about. Latex safe, but not recommended for use with silicone

Uberlube for Sport: Join other athletes using Uberlube as a long lasting anti-chafe. Slather it on so skin glides across itself in a non-greasy, body friendly way.

Uberlube for Hair: Smooth Uberlube over unruly or frizzy hair as a weightless, oil less finishing product that adds a perfect understated sheen to your hair. It consists of the primary ingredient found in many hair smoothers and silkers — silicone — but without any of the synthetic fragrance, preservatives or other bad stuff. Try it solo or mix it into your favorite product.

For more information contact www.Uberlube.com

SYLK

Sylk is the only all-natural personal lubricant made from New Zealand kiwifruit vine extract. SYLK has been sold as a trusted product for over 30 years internationally. In the United States, SYLK is FDA 510(k) Cleared as a Class II Medical Device. SYLK's unique, all-natural formula is designed to mimic the body's natural lubrication, it is pH balanced, condom-compatible (with latex, poly-isoprene, and polyurethane condoms), slippery, and gentle on even the most sensitive skin. Since it is water-based, it will not stain clothes or sheets and is easily washed off. SYLK's proprietary ingredient, the New Zealand Kiwifruit vine extract, is filled with polysaccharides which give the product it's natural, film-like texture/viscosity. SYLK is not made with parabens, hormones, fragrances, or harsh chemicals.

SYLK can be purchased online at www.sylkusa.com and Amazon Prime.

Just Love
Just love is a luxuriously silky, multi-purpose sensual pleasure, massage and moisturizing oil that is great for the skin and safe to use anywhere, anyhow, is a definite favorite. Just Love was developed with top women's health physicians for extremely sensitive skin and bodies, winning several awards in the Natural Health Industry for 'Best New Women's Health' and 'Best New Sexual Health' products. It has great slip and glide, does not dry up and turn sticky and does not need to be washed off. Use as a skin moisturizer head to toe, an edible massage oil, moisturizer for feminine health and hygiene, vaginal dryness and as a lubricant for sensual pleasure and sexual health. 100% Edible, food grade, plant based ingredients. Zero chemicals, preservatives, alcohols, nothing artificial. No water, cheap fillers or sweeteners. Gluten, soy, corn, phytoestrogen free. Comes in 4 deliciously edible organic real fruit flavors and an unflavored version. To purchase please navigate to www.justlove.justpurelife.com

Sexcellence Vaginal Moisturizer:
Compounded for you individually, with hyaluronic acid, vitamin E and aloe, this all natural moisturizer is well received, "no pun intended"

Others include
KY paraben and glycerin free lubricant

Luvena Hybrid Vaginal Moisturizers

Sliquid

Yes

Wet-silicone lubricant for extra slick play

Zestra
Feminine Arousal Fluid (www.zestra.com) may help with orgasm intensity

<u>and latency.</u>

Sexcellence Arousing Cream

007! A compounded clitoral cream to enhance arousal

099! Another choice... not for the faint of heart

These require prescriptions from a sexual medicine specialist. Contact: info@<u>thesexualhealthcenter</u>.com for more information

Books

Barbach L. Pleasures: Women Write Erotica. New York: Harper and Row, 1985.

Heiman JR, LoPiccolo J. Becoming Orgasmic: A Sexual and Personal Growth Program for Women. New York: Prentice Hall, 1988.

Kroll K, Klein EL. Enabling Romance: A Guide to Love, Sex, and Relationships for the Disabled (and the People Who Care About Them). New York: Harmony Books, 1992.

Ladas A, Whipple B, Perry J. The G Spot: And Other Discoveries About Human Sexuality. New York: Holt, 2004.

Laken V, Laken K. Making Love Again: Hope for Couples Facing Loss of Sexual Intimacy. East Sandwich, MA: Ant Hill Press, 2002.

Valins L. When a Woman's Body Says No to Sex: Understanding and Overcoming Vaginismus. New York: Penguin, 1992.

Zilbergeld B. The New Male Sexuality, rev. ed. New York: Bantam, 1999.

Videotapes

Becoming Orgasmic: A Sexual and Personal Growth Program for Women...
and the Men Who Love Them. Chapel Hill, NC: The Sinclair Institute,
1993.

A Man's Guide to Stronger Erections. Chapel Hill, NC: The Sinclair Institute,
1998.

Sex After 50. Ft. Lauderdale, FL: Sex After 50, Inc., 1991.

Informational Resources

International Society of Sexual Medicine: www.ISSM.info

American Association of Sex Educators, Counselors and Therapists www.aasect.org

Endocrinology

American Association of Endocrinologists: www.aace.com

Endocrine Society: www.endo-society.org

Obstetrics/Gynecology

American College of Obstetricians and Gynecologists: www.acog.org

North American Menopausal Society (NAMS): www.menopause.org

Other important websites:

Society for Sex Therapy and Research (SSTAR www.sstarnet.org)

American Association for Marriage and Family Therapy: www.aamft.org :

American Society for Reproductive Medicine: www.asrm.org

Black Women's Health Imperative: www.blackwomenshealth.org

Gay and Lesbian Medical Association www.glma.org

International Society for the Study of Women's Sexual health: www.isswsh.org

The Kinsey Institute: www.kinseyinstitute.org

Lesbian health Research Center: www.lesbianhealthinfo.org

Good Vibrations: www.goodvibes.com

Condomania www.condomania.com

Lesbians   and   Cancer   Resource: Mautner   Project:
www.mautnerproject.org

Other Important Resources

Relizen
We have had great success with Relizen® for the treatment of hot flashes! Relizen is a unique, non-hormonal, non-drug, supplement made from a proprietary blend of flower pollen extract that provides relief of hot flashes and other symptoms of menopause, such as fatigue and moodiness. Recommended by more than 3000 U.S. gynecologists, Relizen has been used safely by more than a million women in Europe where it has been used by gynecologist for more than 15 years. Relizen has been tested in multiple clinical studies, and these studies have shown not only that Relizen is effective, but that it exhibits no hormonal activity and the side effects are no different than those associated with a sugar pill.

Relizen is available directly for purchase at Relizen.com

Revaree
Revaree is a hormone free, paraben free easy to use intravaginal ovule used for vaginal dryness. The active ingredient iis hyaluronic acid. It is backed by multiple clinical studies indicating that it is safe, effective and side-effect free, with results seen in as early as 9 days. Hyaluronic acid has been shown to be just as effective as the leading prescription hormonal creams when it comes to relieving a range of vaginal dryness symptoms, including burning, itching and pain during sex. Additionally, hyaluronic acid can help improve overall vaginal health by maintaining vaginal pH and improving vaginal tissue elasticity, all without hormones.
Revaree is cleared by the FDA and more than one million women across 40 countries have safely used a version of its formulation. Revaree is made from hormone-free hyaluronic acid which has been rigorously studied and shown to be safe and side effect free with no effect on estrogen levels.[2] In addition, it is colorless, odorless and does not contain parabens.

Available at revaree.com.

Imvexxy
Imvexxy is a recently FDA approved ultra low dose estradiol teardrop vaginal insert. It is easy to use, applicator free and effective for vaginal dryness and painful intercourse due to menopause. This requires a prescription from your health care provider.

IntraRosa- A new medication for moderate to severe dyspareunia
Intravaginal DHEA (prasterone) vaginal suppository is the newest medication FDA approved for dyspareunia due to vaginal dryness in menopause. This is used daily and benefit is typically noted within 12

weeks. DHEA is converted in the vagina into estrogen and testosterone, although systemic hormone levels remain unchanged. It has not been tested in the breast cancer patient.

Love Sweat and Tears
How to Keep Romance alive and enjoy intimacy after menopause. Death, taxes and menopause are unavoidable facts of life. Love, Sweat and Tears is a groundbreaking, inspirational and humorous look at the long-taboo subject that will impact both women and men during their lifetimes. For more info regarding viewing opportunities
Visit www.lovesweatandtearsfilm.com

Watch it today on Netflix or buy it on line. It is a must see for both men and women facing the menopausal years.

Pregnitude
Pregnitude is a non-prescription doctor recommended female fertility dietary supplement sold in thousands of leading retail drug stores throughout the US Including Walgreens, CVS and also available through major wholesalers and online retailers.

For more information learn more at Pregnitude.com

Evolution60
Evolution 60 is a newly introduced non-prescription male fertility supplement from the makers of Pregnitude and is sold in selected Walgreens stores and online.

For more information learn more at Evolution60.com

Compounding Pharmacies

Empower Pharmacy

Empower Pharmacy is a 503B registered outsourcing facility that is licensed by the FDA to manufacture custom injectable, oral, transdermal and subcutaneous medications in large quantities to ship directly to clinics and hospitals. We can also compound patient-specific medications that can be customized for the patient to self-administer. Being able to manufacture larger quantities is one reason Empower Pharmacy can offer their catalog of medications at an economical price.

Empower Pharmacy is one of the few facilities licensed in all 50 states to provide both patient-specific and bulk medications for clinic administration. To maintain good FDA standing, Empower Pharmacy adheres to current Good Manufacturing Practices (cGMP) and United States Pharmacopeia (USP) guidelines.

Empower takes immense pride in providing all of our patients with a broad list of wellness products to improve their quality of life. We are devoted in utilizing the most recent technology so that it can build and deliver various wellness products at an affordable cost.

Mission Vision Values

Mission – To be the premier compounding pharmacy and outsourcing facility delivering innovative pharmaceutical solutions to patients and providers.

Vision – Expand access to quality, affordable medications.

Values – People, Quality, Service.

The three core values that guide everything we do:

People: We realize that our people define who we are as a company; therefore, we strive to attain, train, and retain the best in our industry.

Quality: We utilize the latest processes, facilities, and technologies to ensure continuous access to quality medications.

Service: We are here to serve others. We conduct our dealings with honesty and respect for our patients, customers, suppliers, employees, and competitors.

For more information please contact
Empower Pharmacy
5980 W Sam Houston Pkwy N, Suite 300
Houston, TX 77041

www.empowerpharmacy.com
Phone: 832 678 4417
Fax: 832 678 4419
Toll free: 877 562 8577

Innovation Compounding

Hormone balance is essential to a woman's well-being, especially during menopause. Innovation Compounding compounds medicine for each woman's individual needs; including issues related to hormone imbalance, pelvic health, female sexual dysfunction, and more! We believe that proper women's health begins with a balance of the natural hormones to correct other ailments the patient may be experiencing. Along with nutrition, diet, exercise, and stress reduction, supplementation with bioidentical hormones can promote harmony within the women's body. Our passion is to help women bridge the gap between living and living well! Each patient is unique, and so should her medicine! We work closely with 5,000 doctors across the country to help formulate over 60,000 medicines annually to help patients live a high-quality life.

For more information call: http://innovationcompounding.com/patients-vanessis

The Geneveve Treatment

The Geneveve treatment uses the dual-mode, Viveve(R) System to gently heat deep tissue, while cooling and protecting delicate surface tissue with its proprietary cryogen-cooled, monopolar radiofrequency. This heating stimulates the body's natural way to a more youthful tone and resiliency. The single-session treatment typically takes just minutes; no anesthesia is needed, and the patient can get back to her normal routine right away.

Portions of information provided by industry

Who is Michael Krychman?

Michael L. Krychman, MDCM, is the Executive Director of the Southern California Center for Sexual Health and Survivorship Medicine located in Newport Beach California. He is the former Co-Director of The Sexual Medicine and Rehabilitation Program at Memorial Sloan-Kettering Cancer. He also is a clinical sexologist and has completed his Masters in Public Health and Human Sexuality. Dr. Krychman has a degree in Erotology, Sexual Education and Forensic Sexology. Dr. Krychman is also an AASECT certified sexual counselor. He is an Associate Clinical Professor at the University of California Irvine, Division of Gynecological Oncology and the Medical Director of Ann's Clinic, a high-risk program for Breast and Ovarian Cancer Survivors.

His special interests include menopausal health, hormone therapy, sexual pain disorders, and loss of libido, chronic medical illness and its impact on female sexual function as well as breast cancer sexuality. He is a well-known speaker who is featured locally, nationally and internationally. He has published many articles in peer-reviewed journals and has been featured in many scientific journals and lay magazines. Dr. Krychman is an active reviewer for the Journal of Sexual Medicine. He was the Scientific Chairman for the 2010 International Society for the Study of Women's Sexual Health annual educational meeting. He is an active member in good standing in NCBC, NAMS, ISSM, ESSM, ISSWSH and AASECT. He has recently been appointed to the Standard Committee for ISSM and has been a guest professor at the ESSM Sexual Medicine Summer School in Oxford, England. He is a member of the North American Menopause Foundation Board of Directors. He is also on the professional advisory board for the Patty Brisben Foundation and BreastCancer.org. He currently is writing a monthly blog column for breastcancer.org entitled SEX Matters. His radio show: *Sexual Health is General Health* is featured on ReachMD.com

This is Dr. Krychman's 7th book. He has published 6 books including, 100 Questions & Answers for Women *Living with Cancer: A Practical Guide to Female Cancer Survivorship* has been recently published, 100 Questions and Answers about Women's Sexual Wellness and Vitality and Breast cancer Sexuality, Sensuality and Intimacy. He has been featured on the Today show and in the New York Times and US News and World Report World Report, The Wall Street Journal, New York Times, Health Magazine and many others. He was recently named one of Orange County Top Doctors for 2015 and again in 2016 in Menopause, Sexual Dysfunction and Vulvar Pain.

His most important accomplishment is that he is a proud son, loving husband, and the father of two spectacularly outstanding children, Julianna and Russell.

Who is Dr. Alyssa Dweck?

ALYSSA DWECK, MS, MD, FACOG, is a practicing gynecologist in Westchester County, New York. She provides care to women of all ages; she has delivered thousands of babies. A graduate of Barnard College, she has a Masters Degree in Human Nutrition from Columbia University and her Medical Degree from Hahnemann University School of Medicine in Philadelphia, now named Drexel University. Dr. Dweck trained at Lankenau Hospital in Wynnewood, Pennsylvania, where she was Chief Resident in 1994.

Dr. Dweck practices in Mount Kisco, NY and Carmel, NY and admits to Northern Westchester Hospital in Mount Kisco, NY. She has been voted "Top Doctor" in both New York Magazine and in Westchester Magazine. She is proficient in minimally invasive surgery including robotic surgery. She has a special interest and expertise in female sexual health and medical sex therapy. She is an Assistant Clinical Professor in the Department of Obstetrics, Gynecology and Reproductive Science at the Mount Sinai School of Medicine and a consultant at Massachusetts General Hospital, Vincent's Memorial Ob/Gyn Service. She has served on multiple ethics, quality assurance, and peer review committees. She has served on the medical advisory board of Hope's Door, a shelter from Domestic Violence and as a medical consultant for, Stepup-Speakout.org, a web community dedicated to resources and support for breast cancer related lymphedema.

Dr. Dweck is co-author of *V is for Vagina Your A-Z Guide to Periods, Piercings , Pleasures and So Much More* (Ulysses Press 2012) and the newly released *The Complete A to Z for Your V* (Quarto Publishing Group 2017.) She hopes to remove some of the mystery and taboo surrounding many gynecologic issues in a humorous and chatty, but medically sound and up to date "V" guide.

Dr. Dweck is on the Health Advisory Board of Family Circle Magazine and contributed regularly to YM Magazine, in a series called "Paging Dr. Dweck". Dr. Dweck was recently featured on the Today show and Good Day LA. She has also contributed to Cosmopolitan, SHAPE, Family Circle, Health, Women's Health and Girl's Life in print in addition to online sites including Buzzfeed, Vice, PopSugar, Bustle, Refinery29, Health.com, Glamour.com, MORE.com, Foxnews.com, WomensHealthOnline.com, EverydayHealth.com, Parents.com, Sheknows.com, Shape.com, and

PhillyNews.com to name a few. Dr. Dweck speaks regularly and lectures at various Westchester public schools on relevant gynecologic subjects, most recently, Sexually Transmitted Infections. She was a research assistant for Dr. Joyce Brothers. Dr. Dweck lives in Westchester County, NY with her husband. She has two grown sons. She is an accomplished triathlete who also enjoys sports cars and English bulldogs.

More Books by Michael Krychman
Visit Amazon.com or www.thesexualhealthcenter.com

100 Questions & Answers About Life After Breast Cancer
Sensuality, Sexuality, Intimacy

100 Questions & Answers about Questions & Answers About
Human Papilloma Virus (HPV)

100 Questions & Answers About Women's Sexual Wellness And
Vitality: A Practical Guide For The Woman Seeking Sexual
Fulfillment

100 Questions & Answers for Women Living with Cancer: A Practical Guide for Survivorship

100 Questions & Answers About Cervical Cancer

Dx/Rx: Human Papilloma Virus (DX/RX Series)

More By Alyssa Dweck
Visit Amazon.com or www.drdweck.com

V is for Vagina: Your A to Z Guide to Periods, Piercings, Pleasures, and so much more Ulysses Press 2012.

"Sexual Health and Religion: A Primer For The Sexual Health Clinician", Dweck, A., et al Journal of Sexual Medicine, July 2014.

Chapter 23: Female Sexual Dysfunction and Cancer *Sexual Health in the Couple: Management of Sexual Dysfunction in Men and Women*. Lipshultz, L.I. et. al. Springer 2016.

The Complete A to Z for Your V Quarto Publishing Group 2017.
Contact information

Dr. Michael Krychman

The Southern California Center for Sexual Health and Survivorship Medicine:

www.thesexualhealthcenter.com

(949) 764-9300

Dr. Alyssa Dweck

www.drdweck.com

doctordweck@gmail.com

The He said She said duo have been BFFs for years and they are available individually and as a team for personal or professional speaking engagements!

This book has been written and published strictly for informational purposes, and in no way should it be used as a substitute for consultation with professional therapists or physicians. All facts in this book came from scientific publications, personal interviews, published trade books, self-published materials by experts, magazine articles, and the personal practice experiences of the authors, authorities quoted or sources cited. The author's are providing you with information in this work so that you can have the knowledge and can choose, at your own risk, to act on that knowledge. There is no patient physician relationship created with Dr Dweck or Dr Krychman.

Made in the USA
Middletown, DE
08 February 2019